James Hutchison Stirling

Sir William Hamilton

Being the Philosophy of Perception

James Hutchison Stirling

Sir William Hamilton
Being the Philosophy of Perception

ISBN/EAN: 9783337080792

Printed in Europe, USA, Canada, Australia, Japan

Cover: Foto ©ninafisch / pixelio.de

More available books at **www.hansebooks.com**

By the same Author.

Recently published, in 2 vols. 8vo. pp. 1,164, price 28s.

THE SECRET OF HEGEL:

BEING

THE HEGELIAN SYSTEM

IN ORIGIN, PRINCIPLE, FORM, AND MATTER.

OPINIONS OF THE PRESS.

'There can be no question whatever respecting the weight and solidity of Mr. Stirling's exposition. . . . It will mark a period in philosophical transactions, and tend more thoroughly to reveal the tendencies of modern thought in that direction than any other work yet published in this country has done.'
BELL'S MESSENGER.

'Mr. Stirling's learned and laborious endeavours to unveil the mystery of Hegel are entitled to attentive and thoughtful consideration. . . . Mr. Stirling has applied himself to his subject systematically and thoroughly. . . . There can no such complete guide be found in the English language.'
EDINBURGH COURANT.

'This is a most remarkable book in several respects. The Author is, perhaps, the very first in this country who has laboriously and patiently sounded Hegel . . . Unlike any of the commentators of Hegel that we have yet seen, Mr. Stirling can always be understood by an intelligent and attentive reader. He writes as if he wished to make himself plain to the meanest capacity, and he has a facility of language and illustration which lights up the driest and most abstract reasonings of his master.' GLASGOW HERALD.

'A great book has just been published, entitled *The Secret of Hegel*, which, sooner or later, must attract the attention, and influence the conclusions, of true thinkers.' TEMPERANCE SPECTATOR.

'A very elaborate, conscientious, and earnest work. . . . We express our high estimation of the ability and research displayed in it.'
WEEKLY DISPATCH.

'If anything can make Hegel's "complete Logic" acceptable to the English mind, such faith and industry as Mr. Stirling's must succeed. . . . Those who wish to form a complete survey of the great field of German philosophy will do well to study these volumes.' JOHN BULL.

By the same Author.

CRITICAL OPINIONS of '**The Secret of Hegel**'—*continued.*

'We welcome most cordially these volumes. ... A work which is the monument of so much labour, erudition, perseverance, and thought.'
LONDON REVIEW.

'To say that this is by far the most important work written in the English language on any phase of the post-Kantian philosophy of Germany would be saying very little. ... One of the most remarkable works on philosophy that has been seen for years.'
ATHENÆUM.

'The book itself is of much value, especially at the present time. ... It will repay those well who will give the necessary attention to its reading. We have to thank Mr. Stirling for setting these obscure *dicta* in as clear a light as they can be set in, and making them as intelligible as they can be made.'
CHURCHMAN.

'All readers who have the taste and patience necessary for the encountering such tasks will be glad to receive Mr. Stirling's exposition. We have read it with deep interest. It was a very tough task, and he has wrought it in a determined and intelligent manner.'
ECLECTIC REVIEW.

'— Has approached nearer to an intelligible exposition of the Hegelian philosophy than has yet been accomplished in England. ... The Preface a remarkably vigorous and masterful piece of writing—the book able in the highest degree.'
WESTMINSTER REVIEW.

'Mr. Stirling has certainly done much to help the English student. ... He is a writer of power and fire—original, bold, self-reliant, and with a wealth of knowledge and thought that must soon make him distinguished among the teachers of the teachers of this country.'
GLOBE.

'The book deserves a cordial welcome.'
Professor MASSON.

'The whole work is in my view a masterpiece—a *great* book. The style, manner, method, and art of it enchant me—to use a loose expression among general terms. I consider it to be completely successful in what it proposes to do. Its appearance should constitute an era at once in the literary and the philosophical aspect. The ease and fulness of philosophical expression in it— the power and wealth of illustration, comparison, assimilation, analogy, metaphor, literary filling out and accommodation, and finish—are to my mind unique. The labour, the patience—the instinct for truth and for metaphysical tracks and trails—the constant connection with life—the explanatory method of resuming and taking up so that the reader is taught without almost any stress on his own thought—these things continually rouse my admiration and delight. The whole book is colossal—a wonder of work. The style of it is unique in raciness, original force, and utterly unaffected prodigality of wealth —expository, ratiocinative, illustrative, literary, familiar, discursive. The characterisations of the man Hegel are *deliciæ* of literary touch.'
Mr. CUPPLES.

London: LONGMANS, GREEN, and CO. Paternoster Row.

SIR WILLIAM HAMILTON:

BEING

THE PHILOSOPHY OF PERCEPTION.

AN ANALYSIS.

BY

JAMES HUTCHISON STIRLING

AUTHOR OF 'THE SECRET OF HEGEL.'

LONDON:
LONGMANS, GREEN, AND CO.
1865.

The right of translation is reserved.

LONDON
PRINTED BY SPOTTISWOODE AND CO.
NEW-STREET SQUARE

PREFATORY NOTE.

Of the conclusions which, in the 'Secret of Hegel,' I was *occasionally* led to express in reference to the teachings of Sir William Hamilton, I now produce the *Deduction*. Written before the work named (it was written in 1862, and is now re-written principally for the sake of condensation, and always and only from the original materials), this deduction rose from the necessity to examine the productions of my predecessors in the field of German thought. Of these, before this examination, Sir William Hamilton was to me, so to speak, virgin-ground: I had heard of him, but I had not read a single word he had written. I believed what I had heard, nevertheless, and, so believing, approached him—a countryman of my own—with no expectation, no wish, no thought, but to find all that I had heard true. Nor, in a certain sense, did the event prove otherwise: Sir William Hamilton showed at once as a man of infinite acquirement, infinite ability. In a certain other sense, however, the event did prove otherwise, and my expectations were disappointed.

It is to be said, at the same time, that the surprise at my own results, together with the resistance to these results which I met with at the hands of two of Sir William Hamilton's most competent and admiring students, in whose society the relative study was pretty much carried on, threw me so often back on the duty of re-investigation that, in the end, it was impossible for me longer to doubt the truth of my own conclusions.

This deduction is divided into four parts: I. The philosophy of perception, containing as subsections under it—1. Hamilton both presentationist and phenomenalist; 2. The testimony of consciousness, or Hamilton's ὅτι; 3. The analysis of philosophy, or Hamilton's διότι; and 4. The principle of common sense: II. The philosophy of the conditioned, containing as subsections under it—1. The absolute; 2. Hamilton's knowledge of Kant and Hegel; and 3. The law of the conditioned: III. Logic; and, IV. A general conclusion.

Of these parts, I publish now only the first; amounting, perhaps, to about a third of the whole. This part, however, is, so far as Hamilton's activity is concerned, the most important. It will, of itself, probably, suffice to justify, on the whole, the conclusions spoken of as already before the public; and it is

solely with a view to this justification that it *is*
published. The other parts are, for the present,
suppressed, in submission to the temper of the time,
and in consideration of the intervention, on the same
subject, and, as I understand, with similar results, of
my more distinguished contemporary, Mr. Mill.

I am sensible, at the same time, that this partial
publication is, in every point of view but the one
indicated, unjust to myself. I seem to myself to have
discovered in Hamilton a certain vein of disingenuousness that, cruelly unjust to individuals, has probably
caused the retardation of general British philosophy
by, perhaps, a generation; and it is the remaining
parts of my deduction that are, after all, the best fitted
to demonstrate this, and establish grounds for any
indignation which I may have been consequently led
to express—though without the slightest ill-will, of
which, indeed, however adverse to the mischievous
vein concerned, I am entirely unconscious. Really,
grown men, already gray with work, do not take
boyish hatreds at what they examine for the first
time then, and in general interests. Nay, many
of the averments in question occur in those provisional Notes that were intended, in the first instance,
for no eye but my own, and arise, therefore, from a
man who, in presence only of a scientific fact, feels
himself as free in its regard from passion or prejudice
as the air that embraces it, or the light that records it.

Such reasons for regret, then, are not wanting as regards the parts withheld, and certainly, too, there may be something in the exhaustive discussion of all that Hamilton has anywhere said of the Germans (part ii. 2) calculated to be of advantage, and give information, at present. As it is, however, I believe I act for the best in publishing, in the meantime, only the philosophy of perception.

SIR WILLIAM HAMILTON,
&c.

The works of Sir William Hamilton, Logician, present themselves, as is well known, in six volumes of no inconsiderable bulk. Bulk, in this case, need not repel, however; for at the same time that the present inquest has been universal and unexceptive, it has resulted thence that the six volumes stand to the three reviews — 'Perception,' the 'Absolute,' and 'Logic'—pretty much as quantity to quality; so that he who possesses the latter may, with tolerable justice, claim the former also. These reviews, indeed, contain the writer's *stock*, and any study else in Hamilton—unless of a few of the notes to Reid—may be held superfluous.

I.

THE PHILOSOPHY OF PERCEPTION.

In this *stock*—we may say it at once—Perception is the middle-point, and to it, therefore, the present examination directly addresses itself. Perception, indeed, constitutes the middle-point of the entire movement named Scotch Philosophy, and the reason lies in the general object of that movement's originator. Reid, namely, sought to replace the Mediate and Representative Perception of the 'Ideal System' — a perception that asserts itself to perceive, not things without, but ideas within — by the Immediate and Presentative Perception of Common Sense, which believes itself to perceive, on the contrary, not ideas within, but things without. And, if this was the object of Reid, it was equally the object — with but few exceptions (Brown, for example) — of his followers, and, among these, of Hamilton in especial. Hence it was that he (Hamilton) — on the authority of 'consciousness' and with appeal to 'common sense' — opposed to the theory of 'representationism,' or 'cosmothetic idealism,' his own creed of 'presentationism,' or 'natural realism,' 'natural dualism.' This, indeed, is the information of the very first step in Hamilton — information so impossible to mistake, that it is not easy to describe the shock with which we experience the contradiction of the second. It is with this contradiction, then, that we shall open the present discussion.

1. *Hamilton both Presentationist and Phenomenalist.*

We quote at once as follows: —

I hold that Perception is an Immediate or Presentative, not a Mediate or Representative, cognition. (Reid's *Works*, p. 883.) Perception is the faculty presentative or intuitive of the phenomena of the Non-Ego or Matter. (Reid's *Works*, p. 809.) In Perception, mind is immediately cognisant of matter. (Reid's *Works*, p. 755.) A thing is known *immediately* or proximately, when we cognise it *in itself*; *mediately* or *remotely*, when we cognise it *in or through something numerically different from itself.* An immediate cognition, inasmuch as the thing known is *itself presented* to observation, may be called a *presentative*; and inasmuch as the thing presented, is, as it were, *viewed by the mind face to face*, may be called an *intuitive*, cognition. A mediate cognition, inasmuch as the thing known is *held up or mirrored to the mind in a vicarious representation*, may be called a *representative* cognition. (Reid's *Works*, p. 805.) To be known *immediately*, an *object* must be known *in itself*. (*Disc.* p. 50.) Mind and Matter are both equally known to us as existent and in themselves. (*Disc.* p. 52.) Knowledge of mind and matter equally *immediate*. (*Disc.* p. 54.) Consciousness declares our knowledge of material qualities to be intuitive—this the natural conviction of mankind. (*Disc.* p. 55.) *Knowledge* and *existence* are then only convertible when the reality is known *in itself*; for then only can we say, that it is known *because* it exists, and exists *since* it is known. And this constitutes an *immediate, presentative*, or *intuitive* cognition, rigorously so called. (*Disc.* p. 58.) The *external reality itself* constitutes the *immediate* and *only object* of perception. The *very things which we perceive* by our senses do *really exist*. (*Disc.* p. 59.) The *object known* convertible with the *reality existing*. (*Disc.* p. 93-4.) Immediate knowledge of external objects . . . if we hold the doctrine of immediate perception, the necessity of not limiting consciousness to our subjective states. (*Meta.* i. 229.) Consciousness, a knowledge of the object of perception,—meaning by that object the unknown reality itself. (*Meta.* i. 231.) The material reality is the object immediately known in perception. (*Meta.* i. 279.) Those things we immediately perceive are the real things. (*Meta.* i. 289.) In perception we immediately know the external reality in its own qualities, as existing . . . knowledge and existence convertible . . . the reality is known in itself [*bis*] . . . the external reality itself constitutes the immediate and only object of perception. . . . Intuitive or immediate knowledge is that in which there is only one object, and in which that object is known in itself or as existing. In an immediate cognition, the object in consciousness and the object in existence are the same; the *esse intentionale or representativum* coincides with the *esse entitativum*, the two objects both in representative knowledge. (*Meta.* ii. 80, 81, 82, 87, 88, 69.) The Hypothetical Realist [otherwise called also the 'Representationist' or the 'Cosmothetic Idealist'] contends that he is wholly ignorant of things *in themselves*, and that these are known to him, only through a vicarious phenomenon, of which he is conscious in perception;

'Rerumque ignarus, *imagine* gaudet.' (*Disc.* p. 57.) *

The last of these extracts adds the light of the antithesis to that of the thesis so abundantly present in the rest; and only two points, perhaps, give a moment's pause. Firstly, the quotation from page 755 of Reid's *Works* asserts an immediate cognition of matter, while that from page 809 substitutes for matter the phenomena of the same; and in this way the two contradictories of noumenal and phenomenal knowledge would seem to be identified. Secondly, the quotation, *Meta.* i. 231, talks of the object of cognition as the unknown reality itself, and thus, so far as the words go, seems on the part of a presentationist—to whom, necessarily, the reality itself is not unknown—a contradiction in terms. Neither difficulty, however, is of any moment as it stands. The term phenomena is used, not always as in relation to cognition, and so, therefore, as opposed to noumena, but frequently also just as *event* in general; while the phrase *the unknown reality itself* is too plainly a mere allusion to a common parlance of the opposite school, to cause a moment's hesitation. These extracts, then,

* In the above, the italics are Hamilton's own.

will, without difficulty, be received as definitively demonstrative of that appeal to consciousness and common sense,—of that presentationism, realism, dualism,—of that acceptance of the position of Reid generally,—which we have already attributed to Hamilton. Two opinions on the matter, indeed, cannot well be conceived possible: this is Hamilton's overt and publicly known position. Nevertheless, we have now to see, as already hinted, that if, in the extracts above, Hamilton has asserted presentationism and appealed to common sense, he has, in these others below, asserted phenomenalism and appealed to the philosophers,—and this, too, as it would seem, with equal conviction, equal decision:—

Whatever we know is not known as it is, but only as it seems to us to be. (*Meta.* i. 146.) Mind and matter exist to us only in their qualities: and these qualities exist to us only as they are known by us, i. e. as phenomena. (*Disc.* p. 61.) The universe and its contents,—these are known to us, not as they exist, but as our mind is capable of knowing them. (*Meta.* i. 61.) Existence is not cognisable absolutely and in itself, but only in special modes; because these modes can be known only if they stand in a certain relation to our faculties; and because the modes, thus relative to our faculties, are presented to, and known by, the mind only under modifications determined by these faculties themselves. (*Meta.* i. 148.) Although, therefore, existence be only revealed to us in phenomena, and though we can, therefore, have only a relative knowledge either of mind or of matter; still by inference and analogy we may legitimately attempt to rise above the mere appearances which experience and observation afford. (*Meta.* i. 125.) [At page 143 of this volume, he avails himself, in his own support, of the same passages from the Micromégas of Voltaire which he finds quoted by Brown in support of Representationism; and, indeed, Brown in this seems to have reason, for a man with a thousand senses, or even a single additional sense, would have a very different world from ours.] The distinction of two substances (mind and matter) is only inferred from the seeming incompatibility of the two series of phenomena to co-inhere in one, &c.—[and winds up again with]

'Rerumque ignarus, imagine gaudet.' (*Meta.* i. 138.)

To obviate misconception, we may here parenthetically observe, that all we *do* intuitively know of self,—all that we *may* intuitively know of not-self, is only *relative*. Existence *absolutely* and *in itself* is to us as zero; and while nothing *is*, so nothing is *known* to us, except those phases of being which stand in analogy to our faculties of knowledge. These we call *qualities*, *phenomena*, *properties*, &c. When we say, therefore, that a thing is *known in itself*, we mean only that it stands face to face, in direct and immediate relation to the conscious mind; in other words, that, *as existing*, its phenomena form part of the circle of our knowledge,—exist, *since* they are known, and are known *because* they exist. (*Disc.* p. 54.) [From p. 60 of the same work, there follows, for several consecutive pages, a long polemic against 'the principle that the relation of knowledge implies an analogy of existence,' which 'analogy,' nevertheless, the above citation seems to assert.] What we know is not a simple relation [yet in the citation above, it is called 'a direct and immediate relation'] apprehended between the object known and the subject knowing,—but every knowledge is a sum made up of several elements, and the great business of philosophy is to analyse and discriminate these elements, and to determine whence these contributions have been derived. (*Meta.* i. 146.) The sum of our knowledge of the connection of mind and body is, therefore, this,—that the mental modifications are dependent on certain corporeal conditions; but of the nature of these conditions we know nothing. For example, we know, by experience, that the mind perceives only through certain organs of sense, and that, through these different organs, it perceives in a different manner. But whether the senses be instruments, whether they be media, or whether they be only particular outlets to the mind incarcerated in the body,—on all this we can only theorise and conjecture. We have no reason whatever to believe, contrary to the testimony of consciousness, that there is an action or affection of the bodily sense previous to the mental perception; or that the mind only perceives in the head, in consequence of the impression on the organ. On the other hand, we have no reason whatever to doubt the report of consciousness that we actually perceive at the external point of sensation, and that we perceive the material reality—not absolutely and in itself, [however, as he goes on to remark. No:] the total and real object of perception is [he says] the external object under relation to our sense and faculty of cognition. [But it is still] no representation, —no modification of the ego, it is the non-ego modified and relative, it may be, but still the non-ego. For example [he continues], the total object perceived being 12, the external reality may contribute 6, the material sense 3, and the mind 3 [or, as he gives it slightly changed elsewhere, *Meta.* i. 147], the full or adequate object perceived being equal to 12, this amount may be made up of 3 several parts,—of 4, contributed by the object,—of 4, contributed by all that intervenes between the object and the organ,—and of 4, contributed by the living organ itself: this may enable you [he tells his students] to form some rude conjecture of the nature of the object of perception. [Surely, he might have added, and a very rude conjecture, indeed, of an *immediate* perception!] (*Meta.* ii. 128.) Our whole knowledge of mind and of matter is relative,—conditioned,—relatively conditioned. Of things absolutely or in themselves, be they external, be they internal, we know nothing, or know them only as incognisable; and become aware of their incomprehensible existence only as this is indirectly and accidentally revealed to us, through certain qualities related to our faculties of knowledge, and which qualities, again, we cannot think as unconditioned, irrelative, existent in and of themselves. All that we know is therefore phenomenal—phenomenal of the unknown. The philosopher speculating the worlds of matter and of mind, is thus, in a certain sort, only an ignorant admirer. In his contemplation of the universe, the philosopher, indeed, resembles Æneas contemplating the adumbrations on his shield; as it may equally be said of the sage and of the hero,—

'*Miratur; Rerumque ignarus, Imagine gaudet.*'

[Then follow testimonies to the truth of this doctrine from Protagoras, Aristotle, St. Augustin, Boethius, Averroes, Albertus Magnus, Gerson, Leo Hebræus, Melanchthon, Julius Cæsar Scaliger, Francis Piccolomini, Giordano Bruno, Campanella, Bacon, Spinoza, Sir Isaac Newton, and Kant. Of these we quote the following:—] Protagoras: ' Man is [for himself] the measure of all things.' Boethius: ' Omne quod scitur, non ex sua, sed ex comprehendentium, natura cognoscitur.' And (*Meta.* i. 61), ' Quicquid recipitur, recipitur ad modum recipientis.' Leo Hebræus: 'Cognita res a cognoscente, pro viribus ipsius cognoscentis, haud pro rei cognitæ dignitate recipi solet.' Scaliger: ' Nego tibi ullam esse formam nobis notam plene et plane: nostramque scientiam esse umbram in sole [contendo].' And (*Meta.* i. 140): ' Sicut vulpes, elusa a ciconia, lambendo vitreum vas pultem haud attingit: ita nos externa tantum accidentia percipiendo, formas internas non cognoscimus.' Bruno: ' Ita etiam, neque intellectus noster se ipsum in se ipso et res omnes in se ipsis, sed in exteriore quadam specie, simulacro, imagine, figura, signo.' Bacon: ' Informatio sensus semper est ex analogia hominis non ex analogia universi; atque magno prorsus errore asseritur sensum esse mensuram rerum.' Spinoza: ' Mens humana ipsum humanum corpus non cognoscit, nec ipsum existere scit, nisi per ideas affectionum quibus corpus afficitur. Mens se ipsam non cognoscit, nisi quatenus corporis affectionum ideas percipit.' Kant: ' In perception everything is known in conformity to the constitution of our faculty.' [Hamilton adds:] 'And a hundred testimonies to the same truth might be adduced from the philosopher of Kœnigsberg, of whose doctrine it is, in fact, the foundation.' (*Disc.* pp. 643–647.)*

On the question of accuracy here, the reader must understand that he has no room to doubt. Both series of statement occur in Hamilton, and both are perfectly co-extensive and equally precise. Of both, too, the quoted specimens might have been indefinitely augmented, although a tithe of either—so far as conviction is concerned—would probably have sufficed. Neither, if the facts are certain, have we any more reason to doubt the contradiction they involve. The appeal in the one series is not more certainly to common sense, than that in the other is to the philosophers, and the burthen of the one is not more surely noumenalism than that of the other is phenomenalism.

We may remark that we use these terms, noumenalism and phenomenalism, by preference to any others; for, since Kant, they are those that most accurately define the point at issue. To know a noumenon is to know a thing in itself, or as it is; to know a phenomenon is to know a thing in another, or as it seems. This is the distinction concerned, and on its very edge, apply to it what terms we may.

It is the alternatives, then, of this distinction that are equally asserted by Hamilton, and it is on the resultant contradiction that we are now engaged. The first series, for example, runs thus:—

In perception, the thing itself is presented to, and viewed by, the mind, face to face—it is not held up or

---

* The italics in the above are also Hamilton's own.

mirrored to the mind in a vicarious representation. Perception is an immediate and presentative knowledge—it is not mediate or representative—it is intuitive of the non-ego, of matter, of the object in itself, and not in or through something numerically different from itself. Mind and matter are known as existent, immediately and in themselves. Knowledge and existence are convertible. The object known and the reality existing are identical. The external reality itself is the one and only object of perception, and it is known in itself and as existing.

The second series, again, runs thus:—

The object known is not known as it is, but only as it seems—existence is not known absolutely and in itself—observation and experience afford mere appearances—nothing is *known* and nothing *is* but those *phases* of being which stand in analogy to our faculties—whatever we know is not a simple relation but a sum—we know only qualities, phenomena—all that we know is but phenomenal of the unknown—existence absolutely and in itself is to us as zero—things in themselves are incognisable—their existence is incomprehensible, and is only indirectly and accidentally known.

In short, with relation to perception, according to the first series, the external reality—or what is called the *unknown reality*—is itself, and in itself, and as it is, or as it exists, immediately and intuitively (or face to face) presented to the mind. According to the second series, again, the reality itself is not only admittedly *called* unknown, but it admittedly *is* unknown — unknown in itself, unknown as it is, unknown as it exists (presented to the mind, therefore, one would suppose, not only not immediately, not intuitively, not face to face, but simply not at all); and leaving room, consequently, for no knowledge in its, or any, regard that is not of the nature of mere seeming, mere appearance—that is not indirect, accidental, and phenomenal—that is not indirect, accidental, and phenomenal only of what is unknown, incognisable, incomprehensible. Lastly, just to clinch certainty itself here, Hamilton himself, in defining the representationist not to know things in themselves but only in a vicarious phenomenon, would seem directly to identify the position of the representationist with what we can only name his own second position.

It seems, too, but to add the last touch to contradiction here, to observe that Hamilton's action in all this cannot be regarded as wholly inadvertent, but must be considered as at least in some degree conscious. 'To obviate misapprehension,' he says (*Disc.* p. 54), 'we may parenthetically observe'—and the parenthesis occurs in the midst of a profession of the strictest noumenalism—'that all we *do* intuitively know of self, &c., is only *relative*,' &c.* Evidently, therefore, it is not without a certain consciousness that Hamilton scruples not to fling into a single heap the terms of both alternatives at once, or rather even to correct and explain the strict language of noumenalism by the no less strict language of phenomenalism—placing the latter, indeed, as but the defining surrogate of the former. Now we cannot say that our general sense of contradiction, or that our surprise, is in any

---

* See quotation at p. 6, but consult original also.

degree weakened by our perception of this consciousness of Hamilton. Rather, on the contrary, our sense of contradiction and our surprise are thereby very much increased; and this, while we experience in addition both discomfort and offence—discomfort and offence, namely, in consequence of the confusion introduced into well-founded and long-established distinctions by what at least seems the arbitrary caprice of a single individual. Nevertheless, this consciousness of Hamilton being admitted as a fact, our general position is necessarily changed. It becomes our duty, namely, to inquire into Hamilton's actuating reasons, which reasons may be found in the end—despite the confusion that may result—to reconcile contradiction and establish their object.

Why, then, has Hamilton, at the same time that he holds all our knowledge to be phenomenal only, unequivocally asserted presentationism as well?

This question we shall consider presently. It will be well, however, to dwell a moment on some *subordinate* contradictions which, present with, are not unillustrative of, the main one.

Of these the first concerns again Hamilton's already-mentioned consciousness of this main contradiction itself. On this we have to make clear to ourselves that we know of this consciousness only in that we have seen Hamilton expressly cross the two series, or in that we have seen him expressly apply the one in interpretation of the other. This is conclusive as regards a consciousness of the *fact* of the action; it is inconclusive as regards any consciousness of what the action itself *involves*. It seems, indeed, never to have struck Hamilton that presentationism is noumenalism, and therefore the logical contradictory of phenomenalism. Nowhere does he seem aware that he may appear to have committed the contradiction of directly identifying these opposites. Nowhere do we find in him any show of explanation, nowhere any apology, nowhere even an acknowledgment. He seems to have viewed it as a matter of course that he might consistently maintain at once the phenomenalism of the philosophers and the presentationism of Reid. '*To obviate misconception*,' that he should be known simply to *say* so and so, appeared enough to him, even though what he said should be that, when he said noumenalism, he meant phenomenalism—that when he said the one, he meant the other—that when he said *this*, he meant *that!* Here we go round by the rule of *contrairey*. When I say Ay, you say No; and when I say Hold fast, you let go! Boys, we know, play at this game with perfect satisfaction, though, unlike Hamilton, they are not only conscious of the fact of the action, but of its contradiction as well.

But of these subordinate contradictions, perhaps, however small, the most characteristic and striking, as well as the most illustrative of the main one, is this: if, as is readily seen on reference to the preceding quotations, Hamilton, by way of *coup de grâce*, applies to his own enemy, the representationist, the well-known line from the eighth Æneid,

'*Miratur; Rerumque ignarus, Imagine gaudet,*'

en revanche, he applies it—and with a similar representative and summarising force — *twice* to his own self! After this we are not surprised that he should joyfully avail himself of Brown's insight and industry as regards the Micromégas of Voltaire, and should appropriate to himself the warmth of a nest from which, with cuckoo-like regardlessness, he had but just extruded the offspring of its own constructor.

Such another point is this, that, while in the extract (*Disc.* p. 54), he asserts that not only 'nothing is *known*, but nothing *is*, except those phases [i.e. not only is there nothing *known*, but nothing *is*, except *phases*—appearances!] of being which stand in analogy to our faculties of knowledge,' we have but to turn the leaf to find several consecutive pages devoted to a long polemic against 'the principle that the relation of knowledge implies an analogy of existence'!

Very marked contradiction is to be found in the last extract of the second series, whether this extract be considered *for itself*, or in the quotations by which it is so profusely *shored*. The first aspect we pass, as amounting only to that unexceptive and trenchant phenomenalism which constitutes, with reference to Hamilton's professed noumenalism, the main contradiction thus far. But as regards the second aspect, the *shoring* quotations, namely, we shall permit ourselves a word or two.

As is matter of familiar knowledge, the leading industry of Hamilton, in all his most important works, is a polemic—sharp, keen, cutting, headlong—for Reid and against the 'Ideal System,' or for Presentative Realism and against Representative Idealism. Now we have but to think of this polemic, and of the distinguished champions in the opposite ranks whom we recollect to have expressly fallen to the spear of Hamilton, to become all at once even startled by the incongruity and absurdity that seem, in such quotations, almost to mock us. That Sir William Hamilton should make tearful appeal *ad misericordiam* of the very corpses himself had made! That he should summon to the proof the very foes whose bodies are not yet cold on that fierce battle-field which he has just so triumphantly abandoned! That he should seek to re-animate them, and just for that for which he slew them! In a word, that, as phenomenalist, he should be forced to set up what, as noumenalist, he has but just thrown down! It is not easy to set bounds to one's surprise here, at the same time that it is quite impossible to resist the evidence of the fact. The reference to Kant alone is quite conclusive. Kant is not only a representationist—or Kant is not only universally recognised as such, but he is expressly so recognised, expressly so classed, expressly so *fought* by Hamilton. Yet to this same Kant, direct appeal is now made, by this same Hamilton, and in behalf of the very doctrine for which he but this instant hacked and hewed at him! 'Such is the testimony of Kant,' he says, 'and a hundred others to the same truth might be adduced from *the philosopher of Kœnigsberg*, of whose doctrine it is, in fact, the foundation'! No one doubts but a hundred, but a thousand testimonies might be adduced from Kant by the easy process of turning over his pages; but everybody must feel astounded that Hamilton should have even dreamed of an appeal to a single one of them.

Nor, as regards the other authorities, is the incongruity less. In themselves they are generally only less weighty than a Kant, and Hamilton has not been subjected to any difficulty in finding them. To that, indeed, he had but to count the opposite camp—a camp he could not well miss, either, inasmuch as the stream of writers in general directly led to it. This, at all events, is the confession of Reid, who owns to the company of the vulgar, but complete desertion on the part of the philosophers. Now, for the gaining of votes, to count one's enemies — one must at all events acknowledge the gallantry of the expedient. Consider them! Boethius; and 'the object is not known from *its* nature.' Leo Hebraeus; and 'it is not the thing in *its* dignity that is known.' Julius Caesar Scaliger; and 'we only know the shadow, the glass not the contents, only external accidents.' Bruno; and 'we know things, not in themselves, but in another, which other is a species, a simulacrum, an image, a sign.' Bacon; and 'the senses are not adequate to things.' Spinoza; and 'we know ideas only.' In short, the 'Ideal System'!! It is really curious. Did Hamilton, then, wish us to believe that he knew 'ideas' only, that perception is not adequate to things, that we perceive and know but 'signs,' 'images,' 'species,' 'simulacra'? Really, one has to think of Hamilton's reputation, to justify to oneself one's own pains in things so glaring. In the simplest and most gratuitous fashion, indeed, contradiction follows contradiction, and of inconsistency, discrepancy, and confusion, one can find no end. Why, for instance, should Hamilton appeal to — of all men that ever breathed — Protagoras? Why, of all doctrines that ever were enunciated, should it be precisely this heathen's that a disciple of Reid should covet? Protagoras, as everybody knows, was the representative Sophist, or Sceptic, and his doctrine, 'Man is the measure of all things,' is the very 'brief' of that materialistic school which maintains the senses to be the all-in-all both of knowledge and conduct, and with this addition, that, as one man's senses differ from another's, that is true and right for one which is true and right for nobody else. Would Hamilton really have wished us to suppose this principle his, either on the theoretical or the moral side? And again, had he really wished this, why incoherently have made further appeal to Bacon? Protagoras, as quoted by Hamilton, says, 'Man is [for himself] the measure of all things;' and Bacon, as quoted by the same Hamilton, says, 'The information of sense is always from the analogy of man, not from the analogy of the universe, and it is wholly a great error to assert that sense is the measure of all things.' Now to Protagoras 'man' was only the particular *sense* of each particular man: we may say, then, that while Protagoras asserts man or sense to be the measure of all things, Bacon perfectly contra-asserts man or sense not to be the measure of all things. The one assertion is logically the contradictory of the other, and it is eminently characteristic of Hamilton that he should seek to apply both, and in support of one and the same thing. This, indeed, is characteristic — that Hamilton, with such materials before him, should seek to apply two direct logical contradictories, and in support of his own direct logical contradictory to his own self!

But in the sentence from Protagoras there is that intercalated '[for himself]'—did Hamilton intend thus to meet objection, to remove discrepancy? What really could have been his object here, for, if the intercalation is adequate to anything, is it not adequate only to intensify the peculiar, and peculiarly offensive meaning which the phrase conveys and was intended to convey? Then, again, as regards Bacon, why should a Presentationist, a pupil of Reid, &c., &c., rejoice in his authority for the falsity of sense? Were sense false, could perception be true? Has Hamilton forgotten his own words: '*The very things* which we perceive by our senses *do really exist?*' But Bacon, as we have seen, is no exception: we may put the same question as regards the whole of them, seeing that the whole of them simply maintain that Ideal System which Reid and Hamilton believed themselves specially sent to combat and destroy. Really, to love one's enemies is Christian; but, on the part of a philosopher, it is occasionally, we fear, somewhat inconsequent!

'Protagoras, Aristotle, St. Augustin, Boethius, Averroes, Albertus Magnus, Gerson, Leo Hebræus, Melancthon, Julius Cæsar Scaliger, Francis Piccolomini, Giordano Bruno, Campanella, Bacon, Spinoza, Sir Isaac Newton, Kant'—(will the reader forgive me for pointing out in passing that Leo Hebræus must be the *Hebrew Lion*?)—here is a goodly list of names, indeed, and any two of them, say Kant and Aristotle, for example, are quite enough for any single man, but what really at bottom is the value of this whole thing? *For testimony*, is it enough to get a crumb of each of the Doctorum Eruditorum? If we point out that the doctors differ, will you still eagerly demand their crumbs? Nay, if we point out that the crumbs themselves differ, will you still eagerly exclaim, Give, give? Is it enough for you just to get your pages covered with those glittering spiculæ and the more glittering names of which the spiculæ themselves are but the occasions and the pretence? Is there authority then, *so*, in either glittering spicula or glittering name? Or are they not both idle? Strange that Hamilton should have thought so boyish, so very easy, an industry service! To be weak to a quotation that might seem erudite—flauntingly to wear the same, inconsiderate of the occasion:—this is the simple delight of the foreigner in his orders—this is the simple delight of the Negro in his Birmingham buttons. We would, indeed, be just here; but can any man well draw any other or better reflection from that, Sir William Hamilton's long sand-rope of authorities? He calls them a cloud of witnesses, and, folding his hands on his conspicuous erudition the while, he smiles to himself with serene complacency. A cloud of witnesses! Scatter me such clouds, one gleam of sense, one breath of manliness!

It may seem now, that we must have exhausted the

subordinate contradictions present in these extracts; but we feel sure that the reader, should he be inclined to try, has it still in his power to discover more. For our own part, we find ourselves, on turning to the question we left behind us concerning Hamilton's motives for his apparent confusion of noumenalism and phenomenalism, at once encountered by others. These motives, namely, lie in our last two extracts but one, but so that they seem to lie also in very 'nests' of discrepancy. As we have already seen, the former of these extracts asserts knowledge not to be a simple relation between subject and object, but a sum of several elements, which elements it is the business of philosophy to analyse and discriminate. The latter, again, contains such deliverances as these:—It is contrary to the testimony of consciousness to believe an action or affection of the bodily sense previous to the mental perception; we have no reason whatever to doubt the report of consciousness that we actually perceive at the external point of sensation, and that we perceive the material reality,—not a representation, not a modification of the ego,—no, the non-ego itself, modified and relative it may be, but still the non-ego; for example, the total object perceived—this book—being 12, the external reality may contribute 6, the material sense 3, and the mind 3; or the external reality may contribute 4, all that intervenes between the external reality and the organ 4, and the living organ itself 4.

Now, a touch or two will readily reveal the contradictions here. We know from the quotation (*Disc.*

p. 54), for example, that the object stands 'in direct and immediate relation to the conscious mind,' and from quotations of the first series we have abundantly learned that 'the external reality itself is the immediate and *only* object of perception,' and that this object is 'only one.' We learn now, nevertheless, that this immediate and direct relation is a '*sum* of *elements*,' of which elements, constitutive of the *whole* object of perception, the external reality itself is but one. It will suffice to point out this, however; we shall leave it to the reader himself to reconcile, if he can, a direct and immediate (and so, one would think, simple) relation, as well as an object which is described as *one* and *only*—we shall leave it to the reader himself to reconcile both with the *many-ness* and *also-ness* of a sum, and that too, as we shall presently see, a very complicated and peculiar sum.

But, again, it is said, 'mental modifications are dependent on certain corporeal conditions,' 'the mind perceives only through certain organs of sense, and through these *different* organs it perceives in a *different* manner.' Now, if mental modifications *depend* on corporeal *conditions*, surely a certain priority of existence is assigned to the latter by the very nature of the words themselves. Nor is it different with the accompanying allegation that the mind perceives *through* organs, and *differently* through the *different* ones: there too, surely, the very words ascribe priority to the organs, and not only priority, but action as well. (*Difference* of organ produces *difference* of object.) Hamilton, however, has no sooner committed himself to such allegations, than he proceeds, as usual, directly to contradict himself. 'We have no reason whatever,' he says, 'to believe, contrary to the testimony of consciousness, that there is an action or affection of the bodily sense previous to the mental perception; or that the mind only perceives in the head, in consequence of the impression on the organ: whether the senses be instruments, whether they be media, or whether they be only particular outlets to the mind incarcerated in the body,—on all this we can only theorise and conjecture.' Now, if it is to the testimony of consciousness that Hamilton owes these latter statements, one would like to know what testimony he owes those former to. One sees that he is not entitled to doubt as to whether the senses are media, &c., for he has already pronounced them media, and media that operate difference. Perhaps to a mind so constituted as that of Hamilton to perceive *immediately* through *media* is not by any means a contradiction in terms! Even suppose him to perceive 'at the point of contact,' is it so certain that he is not still in presence of a medium—the sensitive spot? Or, on the other aspect, suppose him to perceive the external reality itself—it quite directly, it *all* and it *only*—is he still free to name his perception phenomenal?

Further, Hamilton, as we see from these extracts, rests what noumenalism they contain on two grounds: first, the testimony of consciousness; and second, the analysis and discrimination of philosophy. These grounds we have to see at full again; at present we remark only, firstly, that the testimony of consciousness, though Hamilton's loudest note—a note loud, indeed, only, so to speak, to the deafening and stunning *out* of all opposition—cannot surely be worth much, seeing that, maugre all the mighty things so defiantly ascribed to it, not only the analysis of philosophy is still necessary, but precisely that to and on which consciousness directly testifies and expressly reports remains 'incomprehensible,' 'incognisable,' 'unknown,' 'zero!' And secondly, that, if it is the business of philosophy to analyse and discriminate the elements of this same object of the testimony and report of consciousness, philosophy must be hardly yet fit for its business, not only because what it pretends to analyse and discriminate is admitted by itself to remain, all the same, incomprehensible, incognisable, unknown, zero, but because the actual analysis to which, despite this foregone conclusion of impossibility, it yet very strangely commits itself, is in itself so contradictory, unsatisfactory, and equivocal.

Of this analysis, for example—to dwell here a single moment—there are *two* different estimates actually given in! One is that the external reality is 6, the organ 3, and the mind 3; while the other, retaining the external reality and the organ, though at the new values of 4 each, substitutes for the mind all that intervenes between the reality and the organ—the air presumably—and at a value also of 4! Now, the two estimates differing, we may reasonably conclude that the thing is, as the phrase goes, not quite *reliable* yet. But how different all this is to the standard of common sense which Hamilton himself sets up—how different to his own express and most emphatic allegations elsewhere! How different to all his own 'natural convictions of mankind!' Common sense believes the book it sees just to be the book, and Hamilton asserts existence and cognition to be convertible—asserts the external reality itself to be *only one* object, and this *only one* object to be the *only one* object of perception. Yet here we find that when philosophy is put to '*its business*' by Hamilton, it results that, of the total object perceived, the external reality constitutes only a *half*, perhaps only a *third*! Again, we are told that the perceptive object is no modification of the ego, that it is only the non-ego: yet here *the* business of philosophy actually declares the ego to form a *fourth*, a *third*, or even a *half* of this same object! Philosophy, to be sure, only *says* this—philosophy cannot *do* this. Or, indeed, is any such power still retained among the initiated of the master? Will any descendant of the prophet kindly *show* us either the 6 or the 4 of the external reality—say the book? Either will satisfy us; we shall be quite contented with the 4. That being given us, we cheerfully promise not to say one word of either *organ* or *mind*—that being given us, indeed, we cheerfully promise to be silent even on the *air*! What was so emphatically declared one is now, indeed, triple, even quadruple; but this, too, we shall pass in silence—give us but the external reality itself, be it 6, be it 4, be it 1. If, on the other hand, it should appear that this cannot be done—that the external reality itself, the *substantia nuda*, cannot be shown—unless the book itself, the whole book, and nothing but the book be this—then will it be too much for us to say that, to declare a thing impossible, next, nevertheless, to call this thing the business proper of philosophy, and, lastly, to claim to perform this business, exhibit this thing, but in such manner as only to restore the initial impossibility—on all this it will be enough to say nothing.

Then, again, as regards consciousness, what, after all, are we to think of it? It is a small matter that this so autocratic and infallible consciousness stands in need still of the analysis of philosophy; but surely Hamilton himself would admit that the one and only object of the testimony—of the report of consciousness is the book and nothing but the book; surely he would admit that consciousness as consciousness—for it is to philosophy, and not to consciousness as consciousness (which is common sense, or 'the natural conviction of mankind'), that he attributes the analysis and discrimination—knows not that there is a 3 of the mind, a 4 of the air, or a 3 or 4 of the organ—knows not that what is truly external is, as estimated by Hamilton himself, but $\frac{1}{2}$, or even, perhaps, but $\frac{1}{3}$ of what it discerns—knows not that this which it discerns is really 12! Surely this *is* so. But, if this is so, then consciousness errs. In assuming the whole 12 to be the external reality, which it most undoubtedly does, it errs by at least $\frac{1}{2}$, and by at most $\frac{2}{3}$! But, in such arithmetic, can either error be considered insignificant? Is it at all unfair to suggest, then, that, if consciousness errs in assuming $\frac{2}{3}$ or $\frac{1}{2}$ to be external reality which is not external reality, consciousness may err also in the remainder of the sum, be it ½ or be it only ⅓? And, in such a case, may we not say, then, with Hamilton himself—and the saying is an argument to which he wholly trusts himself— 'if consciousness be confessed to yield a lying evidence in one particular, it cannot be adduced as a credible witness at all,—falsus in uno, falsus in omnibus?'

It may be said that these analyses are only supposititious, only illustrative. We willingly grant the former epithet—we hardly see the pertinence of the latter. Illustrative! Well, it is illustrative of what we shall have perpetually before us throughout the whole of the present inquest—Hamiltonian contradiction, Hamiltonian futility;—this *within*, while *without*, guns, drums, trumpets, gesticulation, and assertion proclaim the advance of an athlete that is to throw a Kant, that is to fling a Hegel. But, grant it to be only an illustration, this illustration, referring to an alleged analysis, must constitute, surely, with the analysis, a legitimate object of discussion. Or if the analysis, indeed, is naught, why the illustration?—or why any talk of it at all?

But let us tear ourselves away from these endless subordinate contradictions, and consider, at last, the question before which we, in effect, stand:—Why has Hamilton, at the same time that he holds all our knowledge to be phenomenal only, unequivocally asserted presentationism as well? This question may be put more fully thus:—What were the reasons which, though unexpressed, were so present to

Hamilton's mind that he perceived no contradiction in, and was never led to offer any apology for, the opposed assertions, now that things in themselves were incomprehensible, incognisable, unknown, zero, and now that they were immediately, intuitively, and face to face, known? Or at shortest:—Why did Hamilton, without sense of contradiction, as it seems, assert at once *knowledge* and *ignorance*—of things in themselves?

Now, as already intimated, the answer here is to be found in our last two extracts but one, and we may state it to run (as if Hamilton spoke) thus:—I do perceive the non-ego, and therefore I am a presentationist; but I only perceive it phenomenally, and therefore I am a phenomenalist. Further, first, I know that I do perceive the non-ego, both by the testimony of consciousness and the analysis of philosophy; and, second, I know myself to perceive only phenomenally, 'Because,' as I say elsewhere, '1°, Existence is not cognisable absolutely and in itself, but only in special *modes*; 2°, Because these modes can be known only if they stand in a certain *relation* to our faculties; and, 3°, Because the modes, thus relative to our faculties, are presented to, and known by, the mind only under *modifications* determined by these faculties themselves.' (*Meta.* i. 148.)

To take the last point in this answer first, or the *modality, relativity,* and *modifiedness* of existence as known—this Hamilton merely asserts. He assumes it to be a fact, an ultimate fact, which, to be admitted, needs only to be understood. He condescends to no rationale: he never dreams of dispute. *Relation, mode,* and *modification* are to him simply self-evident; and he never suspects, in their regard, even the possibility of doubt. This, then, so far, is very loose: it is but a loose appeal to the consciousness of the reader, or an appeal still looser to some presupposed philosophy. Assertion, then, being certainly always equal to assertion, there is the same right to another to assert the substantial, irrelative, and unmodified cognition of existence that there is to Hamilton to assert the contrary. Such assertion of a substantial, irrelative, and unmodified cognition is not far to seek, indeed—if we but return to Hamilton's own *first* series!

As for the testimony of consciousness and the analysis of philosophy, they occur to be considered at full elsewhere; and are here, so far, conceded. That is, we accept the contradiction they offer, and only consider it *as* offered and in itself.

There remains before us now, then, but the single difficulty: How can we possibly understand with Hamilton phenomenal and presentative perception to be one and the same? for, as we know, presentationism is noumenalism. Noumenally to perceive is to perceive a thing in itself, and as it is; phenomenally to perceive is to perceive, on the contrary, a thing as it is in another, and as it seems. These are Hamilton's own definitions of presentationism and representationism. The one, then, is identical with noumenalism and the other with phenomenalism. Of this we are not allowed to doubt; or doubt itself were at once quashed by an instant's reference to Kant. The contradiction of the *two*, then, which to Hamilton are *one*, is sheer.

One might be apt to suspect weakness on the part of Hamilton here—what we might call, perhaps, the weakness of both sides. One might be apt to picture Hamilton, that is, loudly and ostentatiously to take up his position with the 'vulgar;' but, after a while, wistful and penitent, softly to quit his place, quietly to slip over the way, and insinuatingly to whisper the 'philosophers:' I am a phenomenalist all the same! In all probability, however, the facts of the case are differently situated.

That Hamilton was not without satisfaction in his double position we doubt not at all; for, as we have seen, his inadvertence in its regard had no reference whatever to the *fact* of this duplicity. Of that fact, rather, he must be held to have possessed a clear and complete consciousness. No; any inadvertence of Hamilton here concerned, probably, only the burthen of the fact —only the *contradiction* which the peculiar duplicity involved. This we cannot attribute to design—this we must attribute to oversight. And, surely, it is much more natural to believe in the accident of a mistake than in the possibility of Hamilton—with his eyes open—asserting himself to perceive a phenomenon that was also a noumenon. Noumenalism (the 'vulgar') with a *rider* of phenomenalism (the 'philosophers'),—this, indeed, were a device too weak to be imputed to such an intellect. Presentationism, on such an assumption as this, were, to a consciousness fully awake, no longer presentationism at all, nor representationism any longer representationism. Should the external reality be conceived, indeed, to be *pre-*

sented but *in* a phenomenon, then it were not *presented*, it were *represented*. But of this more fully again.

Mistake or no mistake, however, Hamilton's answer is really what the penultimate period above implies: to him the external reality is presented in a phenomenon. However phenomenally wrapt up, the non-ego is actually presented to the ego. Presentation of a phenomenon is Hamilton's conviction: what dominates him is, that the non-ego is *actually there*.

But is, then, the representationist, even in this respect,—and in his answer generally—so very different? To Kant, for example,—in whom representationism certainly culminated—not only was the non-ego present, but the element of a non-ego was absolutely indispensable.*

For proof here, we point, firstly, to the Kritik of Judgment and that harmony of faculties which gives rise to the cognition and emotion of Beauty; and, secondly, to the Kritik of Pure Reason where the element of a non-ego is held to declare itself on occasion of every sensational state whatever.

Kant certainly holds that, though the fact of beauty indicate an adaptation of outer to inner, or of non-ego to ego, and though the fact of sensation indicate the actuality of this outer, of this non-ego, what we know is still really our own state. The non-ego is indispensable antecedent and necessary stimulus or exciting cause, but then it is not this antecedent, this

---

* I hold the second edition of the Kritik of Pure Reason to supersede the first.

stimulus, this cause, but only the consequent, the result, the effect, that the ego knows. This effect is only its own sensuous affection. The non-ego, it is true, is the occasion of this affection, but this intervening affection being all that is in the ego, the non-ego is also, consequently, concealed even by that which alone reveals it.

Now, Hamilton's understanding of this, we remark in passing, is insecure. To him the representationist knows only a 'vicarious phenomenon' in which the object itself is but 'mirrored;' or he knows only a 'vicarious representation,' 'imagine gaudet.' He says (*Meta.* ii. 137), representationism 'supposes that the mind can represent that of which it knows nothing—that of which it is ignorant;' and elsewhere (*Disc.* p. 66) he conceives the cosmothetic idealist, *and Kant as one*, to hold the 'mind either to know the reality of what it represents . . . or to *represent* and *truly* to represent the reality which it does not know.' The object of the representationist would thus appear to be conceived by Hamilton as only an unknown object's likeness, its picture, its portrait, its reflection. But this is an error. *Represent* to the representationist, to Kant, means simply to *stand in lieu of.* Of images Kant does not at all speak; of likeness or unlikeness, he asserts nothing, he denies nothing; mirror-like reflection has no place in his thought; he only says that what he knows is but his own affection, which, though due to a non-ego, and testifying to the existence of the same, cannot add in its regard a single predicate further. That picture on the wall is a representation, a likeness of Pekin; but my perception of the water in this glass (be it a likeness or be it no likeness—of that I know nothing, and likeness is certainly not by any means required) only stands for, and so *represents*, the unknown external thing that *excites* that sentient state of my own known to me, and referred out by me, as water. The skin knows the scratch, it knows nothing of the thorn. Even what the eye knows of the thorn will be found on reflection to be to the eye precisely what the scratch was to the skin, and not by any means the thorn itself. The thorn itself—meaning by the word only the unknown external thing which, acting on my sentiency variously through my special senses, gives rise to the compound perception of my own so named—is certainly there without, undeniably present, an undeniable non-ego that undeniably affects the skin *thus* and the eye *so*; but also an absolutely unknown thing in itself, in regard to which I know only that it does affect the skin *thus* and the eye *so*. On all this, Kant has not left us the slightest room to doubt, and we might quote in proof a thousand passages. For a single instance, see the latter half of the last sentence of § 3 in the Kritik of Pure Reason. To regard the representation of Kant, therefore, as referring to portraiture is simply to *mis-represent*.

To Kant, then, the non-ego is present in perception quite as truly as it is to Hamilton, and Kant, like Hamilton, perceives a phenomenon only: in what, then, are we to conceive their difference to lie? Or how shall we find any difference between 'the unknown thing in itself' of Kant, and the 'incomprehensible, incognisable, unknown thing in itself' of Hamilton, or between the cognition 'as it affects our sentiency' of the one and the cognition 'as it is under relation to our faculties' of the other?

We may conceive, indeed, Hamilton to reply here: My *actually there* is a degree more *there* than the *actually there* of Kant; and *this is the difference.* To Kant, for instance, the non-ego is present only so far as *sensation proper* is concerned; it is not present in *perception proper*; to me, on the other hand, it is present in both. Kant *infers* a non-ego, while I *perceive* one. True, I perceive only phenomenally: true, the external reality, even to the very philosophy that analyses and discriminates its presence, remains incognisable, unknown, zero: still, nevertheless, I know this *presence.* The book we perceive, for example, is made up of, (A) elements due to the external reality itself, (B) elements due to all that intervenes between the book and the organ, (C) elements due to the material sense or organ itself, (D) elements due to the mind; and I call myself a presentationist because, to the analysis of philosophy and the testimony of consciousness, A is actually there—a veritable ingredient, but phenomenally.

Kant, again, is not without such an answer as this: How can you perceive immediately, and intuitively, and face to face, what you declare to be unknown and incognisable? How can you perceive *it* at all? Or how can you perceive what you admit to be present only in a sum, a complex, a compound, a fused σύνολον—*an other*? Your reason *pro* is my reason *con*. What I perceive being A + B + C + D, it is evident that I cannot perceive A itself, or in itself, or intuitively, or face to face, or immediately, or at all. In simple truth, I am a representationist just for this, that, having no means of getting at A, and B, and C, and D, in the disjunct, I am compelled to take them in the conjunct; or just for this, that what I perceive is not A, but A + B + C + D—not the external reality in itself and as it is, but the external reality as it is in another, as it is 'in or through something numerically different from itself.' In short, A *presented* but *in* a phenomenon, is not *pre*sented, it is *re*presented; or if A is only phenomenally *there*, it is also only representatively *there*.

It is useless, Kant may continue, for you here to refer to philosophy, &c., isolating A; for even with this, on your own confession, A remains still a phenomenon. A 'mode,' at first, the faculties have added to it, besides 'relativity,' 'a modification determined by themselves.' It comes forward thus, *still* not in itself, but in or with an other or others; and from these it cannot be separated. It is a triple phenomenon even now, the cube of a phenomenon, but, were it only a simple phenomenon, it were still not in itself, but in an other, in something 'numerically different from itself.' In short, the A which philosophy pretends to analyse and discriminate, is admitted by this same philosophy, not to be A after all, but, as it were $A' + A'' + A'''$, or *mode + relativity + modification*. You are thus still a representationist like myself.

To this Hamilton at once retorts:—The testimony of consciousness is that the non-ego is actually there present, and I accept the testimony of consciousness as infallible;—otherwise God is a deceiver, the universe is a lie, our personality, our immortality, our moral liberty—in fact chaos!

Consciousness, Kant may be allowed to rejoin, is to me, just as it is to you, the seat and the source and the test of truth; but, whereas you merely subjectively assert the testimony of this consciousness to be on your side, I not only similarly subjectively assert that, on the contrary, it is on my side, but I give you my reasons as well.

Reasons! we may conceive the sharp and querulous Hamilton to break in, and have I not given my reasons too? If I have asserted that the testimony of consciousness proves the fact of the case as it has been stated by myself, have I not demonstrated as well that you cannot impeach consciousness in a single instance without equally impeaching it in all—*falsus in uno, falsus in omnibus*; the root of our nature is then a lie, God is a deceiver, our personality, our immortality, our moral liberty, our—our—

Of course, if a man will not hear reason, but just keep doggedly asserting and asserting, we must simply leave him alone. We may conceive the good Kant to retire here, then, with such thoughts in his heart, but muttering to himself, perhaps,—Why, it is just the business of man as man to question consciousness. You, yourself, for the discrimination of A, call in philosophy: you do not trust consciousness as consciousness, and uninstructed, there. You do yourself, in very truth then, thus question consciousness.

At this a light falls on Hamilton, and his doggedness thaws, as he suddenly recalls Kant with, That is true; consciousness, on one aspect, says only A is there, and shows it not; while, on another aspect, it is only philosophy that brings the naked fact in final appeal to consciousness. Consciousness, however, even by this appeal, remains mistress of the situation; and from this situation, consciousness declares the object of its cognition to be not the ego, but 'the non-ego, modified and relative, it may be, but still the non-ego.'

Should Kant have relented and returned, we may conceive him to respond:—It is, at bottom, but by subterfuge, then, that you would claim for *your* consciousness the authority of common consciousness; but of common consciousness, *your* consciousness has yet to abide the question. Meantime, and in reference to your modified non-ego, I may say that an outer object is to you like a parcel of tea tied up in so much sheet-lead and brown paper. The paper is yours, the lead is yours, the string is yours; the tea alone is not yours. You strip off what is yours, the three former then, and you have the tea. But this tea is not yet the *naked* tea; for you admit the naked tea to be still concealed from you by the relativity and modifiedness, &c., fallen on it from your own faculties. After all, it is not the tea you *know*. So little, indeed, is there now left you to know even OF it, that it is hardly worth mentioning, especially in such circumstances. This 'little' itself, however, your own admissions shall now definitively remove.

An apparatus of outer and objective substrates (the primary qualities), to be clothed into the variegated universe by the inner and subjective secondary qualities:—this is your hypothesis, and it is mine. To me, however, these primary qualities have their seat and their source, quite as much, or more than, the secondary, *within*. Not the less, on that account, however, are they to me, as they are to you, really *without*, and *presentant from without*. This peculiarity is due to a demonstrated provision in my space. You yourself identify your primary qualities with space, and you accept my space. Your primary qualities are also, then, *within*. But the primary qualities were the 'little' of a non-ego still left you. Your own admissions, then, have now removed this 'little' into the ego. Your ascription, indeed, of the primary qualities to the non-ego, but resulted from failure to understand my space and your own primary qualities; but of this ascription, in view of my demonstrated space, Occam's razor would compel the recall.

Presentationism, on such a small ground as the *mere assertion* of so scanty and equivocal a non-ego, was always almost absurd in you—so perfect a phenomenalist otherwise; but now the last filament of the already transparent septum has vanished from between us, and we are one—Kant and Hamilton are one—in cosmothetic idealism!

You always knew, not A, but $A + B + C + D$. Even when isolated, A was still a phenomenon, into which you yourself largely entered; or A was not yet known in itself, but only in or as $A' + A'' + A'''$. Of these—and it was not *known*, it was only known *of*—A' was all that remained to you capable of being named outer. This last remnant has now disappeared: your *actually there* and my *actually there* have coalesced and are the same.

As regards our common theory, however, you have been contradictory, misintelligent, imperfect, incomplete, and you still want—possess not a thread of—never attained to a glimpse of a thread of—the innermost net of all, that fine net of the categories that brings the crass nets of space and time, with all their crasser contents, into the punctuality of apperception—into the unity of the I. It is not so certain, then, that I deserved the ostentatious, blind, and somewhat coarse rating you have given me!

In the above discussion, our hypothetical Kant has, in some respects, certainly outgone, not only his own position, but even that of the reader. Nevertheless, the latter, with a look to the future and sufficient intelligence perhaps for the present, may find his own advantage even *so*.

On the whole, we are not allowed now much difficulty in deciding how far Hamilton, in associating presentationism with phenomenalism, was inadvertent, and how far conscious. So far as the latter alternative is concerned again, we may presume that the reasons of his action are now quite plain; and equally plain, probably, the insufficiency of these.

There is still left to surprise us, indeed, the want of

apology on the part of Hamilton—the want of, at least, acknowledgment. We wonder how, while he cuts off, with the most peremptory expression, the most trenchant emphasis, either side from the other, he would, at the same time—almost without naming it—occupy both. Whether, with the 'philosophers,' he folds his hands in 'learned ignorance,' under the shadow of his equivocal phenomenon, or whether he vociferates, with 'the vulgar,' from the platform of his no less equivocal noumenon, that '*the very things* which we perceive by our senses *do really exist*,' and that he shares 'the natural conviction of mankind,' the breadth of clamour with which he calls attention to his position for the time is quite as unmisgiving as it is enormous. It seems to us, indeed, that, while no language can be stronger to say the ink-bottle *is* the ink-bottle, neither can there be any language stronger to say the ink-bottle is *not* the ink-bottle. One might almost suspect Hamilton of taking delight in this utterly abrupt and incommunicable distinction of opposites that were both held. The astonishment it might excite was, possibly, not uncongenial to a mind like his, in which, indeed, a certain procacity, a certain protervity, a certain wilfulness seems always to have place.

Be this as it may, with the deliverances of our hypothetical Kant we may regard the discussion as now terminated, and any assertion of presentationism on the part of Hamilton as now, in his own phrase, summarily truncated.

We may profitably spend, however—just to complete the subject in all its possibilities—one word on this, that, had Hamilton asserted a noumenal knowledge of A (his external reality), and not such phenomenal knowledge as converted it into $A' + A'' + A'''$ (or his mode + his relativity + his modification), we might have been obliged to conclude differently. As concerned A, at least, we should have been forced then to allow him noumenalism, presentationism, if, with regard to B, C, D (or organ, medium, and mind), he could only have claimed for himself phenomenalism. This, too, properly considered, ought, perhaps, really to have been his position. To make A phenomenal, indeed, was but, as we have seen, assertoric, gratuitous, and his own subjective act. Having got the mind into direct contact with matter in the nervous organism, which is the operation peculiar to him, he ought, perhaps, to have announced *simpliciter* his ultimate ὅτι— that the mind now had, and held, and knew matter. To what end still thrust between a tertium quid of phenomenalism? Why still talk of modes, modifications, and relations? *This* has been definitively brought up to *that*, and the *that* is a cognisant element; what is there now any longer to forbid the union? The mode is still the matter, the matter the mode. To call extension, &c., mere modes, and to fancy matter only still an unknown noumenon under these modes,—this is an industry that takes with the left, if it gives with the right. When are we to know noumenally, if not in the position conceived by Hamilton? To suppose the thing in itself absent when its characters are present, is the same absurdity as to suppose the thing in itself present when its characters are absent.

Neither, in such immediacy and directness, is the *relation* any longer a disjunction. Rather, it is now a junction—direct cognition—identification—an act in which the two are one. No less easy is it to perceive that the *modification* attributed to the faculties is superfluous: it is the mind itself that cognises; it is matter itself that is cognised. Here if ever, it is a noumenal A that, ex hypothesi, we possess.

In this way, Hamilton might have consistently asserted a knowledge that was at once noumenal and phenomenal—a knowledge that was *partly* this, and *partly* that; and, through the usual expedient of *limitation* (in which at the same time the difference is no less eternal), he might have enjoyed at last conciliation of the two sides. Yet, again, by his own act, Hamilton has prescinded this advantage; for despite the loud phenomenal cries with which he runs with the hounds, he still definitively holds with the hare, and calls himself, as in formal antagonism to the hounds (or 'philosophers'), a presentationist. In this way, Hamilton had made for himself the contradiction absolute; in this way he had cut off from himself all possibility of retreat along a bridge of limitation, leaving for himself no resource but suspension by either arm across an incommunicable chasm. And so, on his own holding in the face of his own showing, he remains. For Hamilton, if wholly a phenomenalist to us, remains a phenomenalist to himself, that calls himself a presentationist.

In conclusion, thus far, we may remark that the true metaphysic of the subject nowhere finds itself represented in the preceding discussion. The noumenon, if contradictory, is also essential, to the phenomenon. Both are: either is impossible without the other. The noumenon is identity, the phenomenon difference. The noumenon is the one, the phenomenon the many. The noumenon is the *an sich*, the phenomenon the *für sich*. Noumenon and phenomenon are indissolubly one—a one in trinity. This, however, despite his *confusion* of both, or even in his confusion of both, is a position unknown to Hamilton, and far beyond him. To Hamilton, in fact, his own principles were such that, had he fairly caught the antithesis of noumenon and phenomenon, he would have been compelled to have applied to it his own incessant instrument of infallible divorce—the excluded middle; he would have been compelled to say, noumenon and phenomenon being logical contradictories, both cannot possibly be true, but one must. Instead of this application, however, of what—on the model of Occam's razor—we may be allowed to name Hamilton's wedge, he has, as it were in defiance of his own ordinary principles, produced that incoherent and untenable phenomenal presentationism of his, which, as Hegel would say, is 'neither fish nor fowl,' but a miserable *Gebräu*, a miserable jumble of mere partial glances (*each* bright enough, perhaps), in a confused multiplicity of directions. This confusion is evident at once in the two standards to which Hamilton appeals: if it is to ordinary consciousness he trusts for decision, it is absurd for him to advance to philosophy; and if he has once advanced to the latter, it is impossible for him to return to the former. The harness of phenomenalism once worn on the stage of philosophy, as that stage was constituted to himself, could never be put off for the naked skin of noumenalism. From that stage, indeed, we can say that Hamilton was quite unjustifiable in blindly tearing up the ancient landmarks, in shaking together the well-grounded and long-established distinctions of history, and in confounding in a common heap two perfectly separate and distinct vocabularies. The discrimina of a thing in itself, and of a thing as it seems, pervade philosophy, and they are not rashly to be effaced by the ipse dixit of even such a man as Hamilton. Nor is this less to be said from the newest and latest metaphysical position; for to it the distinctions are no less true and necessary than the dialectical reflexion by which they are, in the end, identified. Surely, then, the words, 'Very arbitrarily and, in fact, very abusively perverted and contorted,' so familiar, probably, to the indignation of many, as applied by Hamilton to the unoffending Kant—surely, these words may now, with even-handed justice, be retorted on his own offending and unprovoked self. Wedge of Hamilton—razor of Occam! it would probably have been fortunate for the former himself, had he applied here for his own conviction, if also for his own confusion, either wedge or razor.

We turn now to the consideration of what we have hitherto, on the whole, granted—the testimony of consciousness, and the analysis of philosophy.

2. *The Testimony of Consciousness; or Hamilton's* ὅτι.

We begin with the extracts on which our reasonings and conclusions found:—

Aristotle regarded consciousness, not as a particular faculty, but as the universal condition of intelligence. . . . Reid and Stewart again hold that 'the peculiar object of consciousness is, the operations of the other faculties themselves, to the exclusion of their objects.' . . . [Hamilton, as if with Aristotle, and against Reid and Stewart, maintains] It is impossible, in the *first* place, to discriminate consciousness from all the other cognitive faculties, or to discriminate any one of these from consciousness; and in the *second*, to conceive a faculty cognisant of the various mental operations without being also cognisant of their several objects. (*Disc.* p. 47.) Let consciousness, therefore, remain one and indivisible, comprehending all the modifications—all the phenomena—of the thinking subject. (*Meta.* i. 183.) To limit consciousness to a cognisance of self is to deprive it of the power of distinguishing external objects from each other, and even of the power of discriminating the ego and the non-ego. (*Meta.* i. 204.) If consciousness has for its objects the cognitive operations, it must know these operations, and, as it knows these operations, it must know their objects. (*Meta.* i. 208 9.) How is it possible that we can be conscious of an operation of perception, unless consciousness be co-extensive with that act, and how can it be co-extensive with the act and not also conversant with its object? (*Meta.* i. 228.) Consciousness constitutes, or is co-extensive with, all our faculties of knowledge. (*Meta.* ii. 10.) Perception the consciousness of external objects. (*Meta.* ii. 28.) Conscious of the inkstand. (*Meta.* i. 228.) That Reid should hold consciousness to be applicable to the act, but not to the object, of perception is suicidal of his great doctrine of our immediate knowledge of the external world. (*Meta.* i. 227.) His (Reid's) error of commission in discriminating *conscious-*

ness as a special faculty, and his error of omission in not discriminating *intuitive* from *representative* knowledge — a distinction without which his peculiar philosophy is naught — have contributed to render his doctrine of the intellectual faculties prolix, vacillating, perplexed, and sometimes even contradictory. (*Disc.* p. 46.)

To ask, therefore, a *reason* for the possibility of our intuition of external things, above the *fact* of its reality, as given in our perceptive consciousness, betrays, as Aristotle has truly said, 'an imbecility of the reasoning principle itself.' (*Disc.* p. 63.) As ultimate, it is a fact inexplicable.... It can only be disproved by proving the mendacity of consciousness.... Belying consciousness, it belies and so annihilates itself.... The truth of consciousness is the condition of the possibility of all knowledge. (*Disc.* p. 64.) That we cannot show forth *how* the mind is capable of knowing something different from self, is no reason to doubt *that* it is so capable. Every *how* (διότι) rests ultimately on a *that* (ὅτι). (*Disc.* p. 63.) Consciousness is the fountain of all comprehensibility and illustration; but *as such*, cannot be itself illustrated or comprehended. (*Disc.* p. 63.) The Presentationist admits the veracity, the Representationist postulates the falsehood, of that principle, which can alone confer on this incomprehensible foundation the character of truth.... Consciousness must be held veracious, or philosophy is *felo de se*. (*Meta.* i. 265.) If consciousness, however, were confessed to yield a lying evidence in one particular, it could not be adduced as a credible witness at all: — *Falsus in uno, falsus in omnibus*. (*Disc.* p. 88.) By the very act of refusing any one datum of consciousness, philosophy invalidates the whole credibility of consciousness.... The refusal to accept the fact of the duality of consciousness, is virtually an act of philosophical suicide. (*Meta.* i. 299.) If Kant attempts to philosophise, he must assert the possibility of philosophy. But the possibility of philosophy supposes the veracity of consciousness; ... therefore, in disputing the testimony of consciousness, Kant disputes the possibility of philosophy, and, consequently, reduces his own attempts at philosophising to absurdity. (*Meta.* i. 374.)

The object of this writing cannot well be misunderstood. One sees at once that Hamilton—with no will but the subversion of the Representationist and the establishment of himself, and with never a dream but success—is wholly engrossed with two operations only. The first of these introduces mind into the actual presence of matter, and the second declares the resultant report of mind to be necessarily true. Consciousness, he says, can state no falsehood; but consciousness asserts the fact of immediate contact with an externality different from itself, therefore such externality *is*. The testimony is direct, the testimony is unimpeachable. The witness was *there*, the witness *cannot lie*. From antecedents so clear, there is an irresistible consequent—the adoption of the report.

It is evident, too, that to Hamilton the one antecedent is as indispensable as the other: they form together, indeed, but a conjunct tally: they are this tally's complementary pieces; both are equally necessary;—they complete and perfect each other.

As regards the first, we see that direct presence, actual contact, is a *sine qua non*. Discontinuity is never for a moment to be thought of. The slightest gap, the slightest interval, were a breach irreparable, a chasm of despair. The two extremes must meet; the two terms must be accurately conjoined. Mind must actually reach up and out to externality—mind must actually touch externality. To know of it through any intermediation of means is an expedient

—an accommodation—quite to be rejected. That mind should be able to *say*, mind must be able to *feel*. Unless it touch, how can it believe? Hamilton, very certainly, is with his whole conviction here; and he never doubts but that his reader is with him. Consciousness must be co-extensive with perception: this is to him—this must plainly be to all—the preliminary postulate.

On the second expedient, however, it is, that Hamilton, we doubt not, values himself most. It is not enough, he sees, to place externality, as it were, in the clutch of consciousness. However direct the clutch, consciousness may in itself be still incompetent to speak. It is not enough to give consciousness opportunity, consciousness must be found in capacity as well. Any man can look, it is only the expert that can see. This, then, is Hamilton's further operation: if, in the first instance, the witness was proved present, he is now, in the second, proved competent.

Hamilton has long been aware of the inconveniences of *sense*. What are called its subreptions, its mistakes, blunders, errors—: these, hitherto, to the presentationist have been, as it were, the very ghosts that haunted him — troublesome importunates that would not be laid, chant he what exorcism he might. This Hamilton knows well, and this he would annul, or this at least he would *go round*. Now it is always the stir and strike of certain machinery that has raised these ghosts, the stir and strike of the machinery of sense, that is. *Process* is the word, in fact. Process is the single sign, the proof, which, shown to the presentationist, has hitherto insured his instant retreat. It is the roundabout of steps, says Hamilton, which, offering opportunity of analysis, constitutes our whole difficulty. This we must get rid of—*steps* we must efface—*inter*mediation we must thrust from before us, and set down *imm*ediation instead. Process is the presentationist's impossibility—process there must be none.

But again, says Hamilton, not only has it been usual to assert process, but it has been equally usual to refuse to believe what consciousness might say. Now would we establish a direct cognition of externality, not only must we deny the process which has hitherto been assumed, but we must deny also, what always hitherto has likewise been assumed, the right on our part at all to question consciousness. In short, it must be ours to maintain that consciousness clutches externality, that consciousness says so, and that consciousness cannot lie.

It is not difficult to see that, with these concessions, Hamilton has a won game before him. If consciousness supply a direct report, and if consciousness cannot be questioned, then presentationism is inevitable. We doubt not, then, that Hamilton, on the whole, must have often enough surveyed with complacency his own success thus far. Nor can we well *over*estimate the gallantry of the logical *coup de main*, of the logical surprise displayed in every circumstance of his extraordinary argumentation. We readily grant to Hamilton that consciousness must be co-extensive with perception, and we cannot deny this same consciousness to be the ultimate standard of appeal. No sooner do we admit as much, however, than, by an instant sleight of hand, that, under a cover of words, would evade detection, we are astonished into the belief that consciousness and perception are numerically one—nay, by a still more rapid sleight of hand, we are astonished into the belief that consciousness cannot at all be questioned—neither in any function, nor on any occasion, nor at any time.

All now, then, is changed, says Hamilton; it is no longer with perception, it is no longer with sense that we have at all to do. *Organs*—with all their blunders, all their subreptions—have disappeared. As said, the ghosts are laid. It is now with consciousness we have to do, and with consciousness alone. But consciousness is not sense. You cannot dispute consciousness. If you do, it is at once tainted throughout, and it and you and all of us are logically defunct, and there is an end of everything. Take consciousness, but take it wholly, and there is an external world. Reject a tittle of it, and you annihilate your own self and the whole business you follow.

But the mere jugglery, the mere logical blind show of this, must be held all the time as quite conspicuous. The subreptions of sense, plainly, if covered, are not by any means removed; and it is equally plain that it is either an extraordinary self-delusion, or a no less extraordinary abuse of speech, to aver that the facts of consciousness cannot be questioned.

Sir William Hamilton has, in this country, been proclaimed the greatest logician since Aristotle, nevertheless it is certain that he has filled—'prince of philosophers,' and prince of logicians, as he may be—the most important sections of his most important works with the elaborate enunciation of a simple fallacy. This fallacy is the *fallacia accidentis*, and on both of its sides. Whether it is reasoned that, perception being consciousness, consciousness is perception, or that, consciousness being inviolable, perception is inviolable, Hamilton commits indeed this technical error. It is perfectly true, for example, that perception is consciousness; but it is wholly untrue to aver that consciousness is perception—in the sense that all consciousness is perception. When consciousness is spoken of in reference to the cognition of external objects, it is consciousness in the form of perception, it is consciousness *secundum quid*, or, as Hamilton himself might say it, it is only *some* consciousness that is meant. Again, when it is affirmed that consciousness is inviolable, the consciousness implied is universal consciousness, not consciousness *secundum quid*, but consciousness *simpliciter*. But we cannot reason, whether from the essential to the accidental, or from the accidental to the essential, without the risk of committing sophisms. Thus to assert, with Hamilton, that, perception being consciousness, what is true of perception is true of consciousness, is to commit the fallacy of reasoning *à dicto secundum quid ad dictum simpliciter*; while, again, to assert, with Hamilton, that, consciousness being perception, what is true of consciousness is true of perception, is to commit the converse fallacy of reasoning *à dicto simpliciter ad dictum secundum quid*.

Hamilton's general syllogism here, in fact, seems pretty much this:—Consciousness is inviolable; but perception is consciousness; therefore, perception is inviolable. Now here the middle term is consciousness; but, in the major proposition, it is universal consciousness, consciousness *simpliciter*; while, in the minor, it is a particular consciousness, consciousness *secundum quid*, or only *some* consciousness. In this way, then, the syllogism contains a quaternion of terms; or there are two middle terms, and thus, the extremes not being compared with the same thing, the conclusion is false. Special consciousness is, in short, not universal consciousness, and, contrary to the dictum of Hamilton, both must be accurately discriminated. We may legitimately express some surprise, then, at the simple manner in which a professed logician has technically committed himself. Remembering, indeed, that Hamilton was not only prince of philosophers but high priest of the Quantification of the Predicate, we might, by pointing out that this his own operation was the single necessity in the case before us, have brought home to him his error through neglect of the same, in a manner much more keen and cruel. This will appear at once if the true proposition, perception is consciousness, be converted not *per accidens*, not through quantification of the predicate, but *simpliciter*, into the false proposition, consciousness is perception. All perception is only some consciousness, only some consciousness is all perception.

Hamilton's *presto* trick is not, then, so glorious for him after all. Fancy such reasoning as this:—Consciousness is perception; but memory is consciousness; therefore memory is perception! Yet to such reasoning we have a perfect warrant in the procedure of Sir William Hamilton. And by such reasoning is there any difference whatever that could not be identified with its opposite—so far, at least, as consciousness and consciousnesses are concerned?

It is not to escape notice either, that the identification of consciousness with perception does not remove the difficulty of how perception, constituted and conditioned as it is, can possibly be conceived capable of a direct cognition of external things. Call it consciousness if you will, it is still a process consisting of sundry stages and steps which afford us a variety of occasions for instituting experiments to try it and test it. Perception is consciousness, and sight is perception; but there is nothing in this statement to preclude us from the examination of the process of vision, both physiologically and psychologically; and if the results of this examination tend to show the impossibility of any immediate knowledge, through sight, of any outward object, and, moreover, should this result repeat itself in the case of all the other senses, it will be quite in vain for Sir William Hamilton to call out, even with his most peremptory pretentiousness, Consciousness, consciousness; for it is quite competent to us to call out, equally peremptorily, equally authoritatively, Sight, sight,—hearing, hearing,—touch, touch; for each of these is consciousness, and each of these is at the same time capable of a formal investigation.

It is possible that Hamilton might reply here, But you fail to see that I speak of an ultimate fact of consciousness. By no means, we may rejoin; we know very well that you name the general fact in perception an ultimate fact of consciousness; but consciousness here is not consciousness *simpliciter*, but consciousness *secundum quid*; it is still perception, and we admit, if you will, that the ultimate, and universal, and, *pro tanto*, necessary fact of perception is the cognition of something different from self; but it is still competent to consciousness *qua* consciousness, to transcend perception *qua* perception,—to begin where perception left off, and carry up or out the ultimate fact of *perception* into a higher and very different fact of *its own*. Nay, we may say that the special business of consciousness is to carry the outer fact of perception up or in to its own inner truth. Were we to stay by perception, we were but brutes: *our* business is to think, and to think is—in so many words—just to transcend perception. In more intelligible language, it is the business of consciousness to examine all special consciousnesses that may be submitted to it; and among these perception finds itself, and finds itself, too, in its own nature so peculiarly constituted, that there is no other special consciousness so well adapted for the inquisition of general consciousness as it is. By the very phrase, ultimate fact, Hamilton, indeed, just refutes his own case; for it implies a foregone process that has pronounced it ultimate; and, implying process, it implies also a possibility of examining the same, even beyond the arbitrary term of his own *ipse dixit*.

We may remark, too, that the nature of this assumed ultimate fact of Hamilton's does not at all lessen the difficulty of how such substances as mind and matter can come into relation at all. Nor is it to any other motive than a desire to lessen this difficulty, that we can attribute the identification of consciousness with perception on the part of Hamilton, as well as his general attempt to reduce all the senses to that of direct contact—touch. In this way, too, we see that, despite his clamour of an ultimate fact, Hamilton is really obliged tacitly to admit the claims of reason and reasoning, and the demands of explanation.

It is possible, then, almost directly to negative every single statement of Hamilton's in the extracts with which we set out, and to which the reader will, perhaps, kindly consent to turn back a moment. As regards Aristotle, for example, we can see that his doctrine is simply that of universal mankind, and that the doctrine of Reid and Stewart by no means differs. Reid is not guilty of an 'error of commission' in discriminating consciousness as a special faculty. Consciousness is to Reid, as it is to Aristotle, and everybody else unless Hamilton, *the genus*, while perception and the rest are but the *species*. It is but a very unfair accentuation of certain words, which extends but a plausible pretext to Hamilton to speak differently. The truth of the matter is, that of all philosophers, and of all mankind, Hamilton is the only one who has converted consciousness into a special faculty—perception. Against which conversion, we again assert that it *is* possible to discriminate consciousness from the special faculties, as these from it.

Then we *do* perceive, and it is perfectly natural for us to inquire *how* we perceive, let us 'betray so, as Aristotle has truly said, an imbecility of the reasoning principle itself,'—let us betray this for thinking so if we must, but we will console ourselves that this *spicula* of Aristotle, however ornamental to Hamilton, has been probably wrested from its true connexion, and if not, that, as it stands, it is sufficiently valueless. Again, the so-called fact of perception is *not* ultimate: there are steps *to* it, there are steps *from* it. Perception is *not* inviolable; and, in a certain sense, consciousness itself is *not* inviolable. Lastly, the representationist does *not* postulate the falsehood of consciousness. These statements pretty well exhaust the burthen of our extracts, though it would be quite possible to carry the negative into the particular more deeply still.

Consciousness is veracious; consciousness is not mendacious; the facts of consciousness must be accepted; consciousness is our ultimate standard; in order to try consciousness another consciousness were demanded; the facts of consciousness are mutually congruent and coherent, else consciousness is itself false, and the whole edifice of knowledge—society itself—topples; the root of nature is a lie; God is a deceiver; unconditional scepticism is the melancholy result; our personality, our immortality, our moral liberty—in short, 'man is the dream of a shadow,' 'God is the dream of that dream!' No reader of Hamilton but knows these utterances well. How constantly, how unexceptively they are repeated! yet the pole on which they turn, all of them, is a sophism, a fallacy 'probably without a parallel,' as Hamilton himself says of Brown, 'in the whole history of philosophy, and this portentous error is prolific—*Chimæra chimæram parit.* Were the evidence of the mistake less unambiguous we should be disposed rather to question our own perspicacity than to tax so subtle an intellect with so gross a blunder.' (*Disc.* p. 57.) But the evidence is not ambiguous. Hamilton has started with the *fallacia accidentis,* and entangled himself in error ever the deeper the further. Why, were consciousness inviolable in the sense in which it must be understood to legitimate the conclusion of Hamilton in regard to the evidence of perception, then the tale of history is a dream, for that whole tale is but the transcendence of error after error, and these errors were the errors of consciousness. For what are all our reformatories, refuges, asylums,—for what are missions,—to what use schools,—if special need not the correction of universal consciousness? History! what is it else than this? What is it else than the transcendence morally, æsthetically, and intellectually of sense? *Morally,* for example, the *good* is now above the *personal*, and *æsthetically* the *beautiful* is above the *sapid*: but was either so, when mankind belched the acorn? Then, *intellectually*, what original facts of consciousness, so far as sense—so far as perception is consciousness, have not been changed? The earth is no longer a plane; the firmament over it has gone into immensity,—its lights are worlds. History has, in a manner, fixed the sun; and yet that in the morning he rises in the east, and in the evening sets in the west, if false to intellect is true to sense, if false to *consciousness*, is true to *perception*.

Nay, why talk of history, when the daily experience of each of us can tell but the self-same tale? For what *is* experience?—what but a *later* fact of consciousness transcending (i. e. falsifying) an earlier one? The child is conscious that there is a crooked stick in the water; the man is conscious that the very same stick is straight. This same man, again, is conscious that it is the rose is red, the sugar sweet, &c.; but the philosopher, and, as we shall see presently, even such a philosopher as Hamilton, is conscious that all this is otherwise. Experience, then, is but a mutation of the facts of consciousness, and the assumption of an inviolability of consciousness (in order to counteract and nullify this mutation) would, if followed out to its legitimate consequences, terminate in an intellectual stand-still and a moral quietism destructive of philosophy, destructive of society, destructive of life. In a certain sense, indeed, had consciousness been inviolable, the universe had never been,—God had been but bare identity; and difference there had been none. For the truth is even that which is viewed by Hamilton as an absurdity: in very truth there is a consciousness beyond consciousness; and it is the function of consciousness, though itself infallible, inviolable, and veracious as nothing else is or can be, to test and try and question consciousness to the uttermost. Consciousness stands under consciousness, and the vocation of consciousness is simply infinitely to transcend itself. In a word, the business of consciousness is to think, and to think is to transcend perception—to think is to transcend thought itself. Nor have we a warrant to think otherwise of the consciousness, otherwise of the thought of God; for He has revealed Himself to us as *a Spirit* in whose *image* the spirit of man is made.

What is loudest in Hamilton, however, is his rude and deafening denial—to the cosmothetic idealist (say) —of any right thus to question consciousness. Consciousness, he perpetually exclaims, is imperative as to the existence of self and not self; and consciousness cannot be proved mendacious without annihilating philosophy, and so sisting the whole business at a blow; for consciousness being proved false anywhere, can be trusted nowhere. The cosmothetic idealist, for his part, we may conceive as always on the point of beginning with, But let us *look* at the fact, when his voice is instantly drowned by a repetition of the clamour about veracious, veracious, mendacious, mendacious, &c. Nevertheless, it is not discrepant, from what we know of Hamilton already, that he should—at his own time—be actually found to admit the legitimacy of a subjection of the facts of consciousness to scrutiny and question. That is as much as to say, that Hamilton at once forbids and commands—the examination of consciousness. On the latter head, for example, we find him saying (*Disc.* p. 87): 'Psychology is only *a developed consciousness*, that is, a *scientific evolution of the facts* of which consciousness is the guarantee and revelation.'

We may conceive the cosmothetic idealist, then, to recover heart here, and to call out cheerily, That is it, that is just what I want—consciousness is, as you say, both revelation and guarantee; but, as you say also, we can develop consciousness, we can accomplish a scientific evolution of its facts; and, perhaps, this development and evolution will not be found to stop precisely at the spot you indicate, if you will but have the goodness to listen to me a moment.

'Philosophy' (*Meta.* i. 277) 'is only a systematic evolution of the contents of consciousness by the instrumentality of consciousness.' This, again, is but the same admission, and Hamilton said no less, indeed, when he told us formerly that, ' by inference and analogy, we may legitimately attempt to rise above the mere appearances which experience and observation afford.' It is in the same sense that we find him (*Meta.* i. 121) describing 'the three grand questions of philosophy' as '1°, phenomena (the facts) in general; 2°, their laws; 3°, inferences—results.' Why, these three grand questions of facts, laws, and inferences, are just the points which Hamilton's opponent would inquire into, if he (Hamilton), leaving off his cry of ultimate and ultimate, would but let him. The cosmothetic idealist would be glad, we may suppose, were he but allowed to act as Hamilton himself implies when he avers that 'the great business of philosophy is to analyse and discriminate.'

But the cosmothetic idealist, on the whole, has been treated with positive cruelty by Hamilton. How often, for example, do we not find the latter exciting the former's hopes, leading him (the former), in what appears his own (the former's) way, directly up to what again appears his own (the former's) problem; but, when the very point of promise has been reached, suddenly deserting him again with, 'The facts of consciousness?' Thus, for instance (*Meta.* i. 273), he 'cannot but regard Stewart's assertion—that the present existence of the phenomena of consciousness, and the reality of that to which these phenomena bear witness, rest on a foundation *equally solid*—as wholly untenable,' and he exclaims (*Meta.* i. 276), 'It is not the *reality* of consciousness that we have to *prove*, but its *veracity* or—*the authority of the facts of consciousness as evidence of something beyond themselves.*' Then (*Meta.* i. 275) he allows himself, accepting 'the facts given in the act of consciousness itself,' to doubt 'the facts which consciousness does not at once give, but to the reality of which it only bears evidence;' nay, he allows himself to be able, '*without self-contradiction*, to maintain that what he is compelled to view as the phenomena of something different from himself is nevertheless (unknown to himself) only a modification of his own mind.' A similar avowal is this (Reid's *Works*, p. 129, note), 'I cannot doubt that I am conscious of it (the rose) as something different from self; but whether it have, indeed, any reality beyond my mind—whether the not-self be not in truth only *self*—that I may philosophically question.' Now all this is just as if the cosmothetic idealist himself were speaking, and with all this we may conceive that dejected individual highly gratified and charmed. Only one step further, however, and he will find every new hope suddenly quashed again beneath the old assertion of 'the facts,' and 'the facts.' These facts he had certainly been encouraged to question, but the instant he would attempt to act on the encouragement, he is stopped, panic-stricken, by the significant threat of the encourager himself, who (*Meta*. i. 277) assures him, 'This can be done only by showing that consciousness tells different tales—that its evidence is contradictory—that its data are repugnant;—*but this no sceptic has ever yet been able to do!*'

No; let the cosmothetic idealist who reads Hamilton conceive at times what hopes he may, he will find ever in the end that, at the very moment of fruition, they are suddenly dissipated by the cold reassertion (*Meta*. i. 278) of 'the fact to which consciousness testifies,—that the object of which we are conscious in perception is the external reality as existing, and not merely its representation in the percipient mind.' The peculiar procedure which we would here signalise finds, perhaps, its best illustration in the following passage from Reid's *Works*, p. 744:—

It is, however, possible for us to suppose, without our

supposition at least being *felo-de-se*, that, though *given as* a non-ego, the object may, *in reality*, be only a *representation* of a *non-ego*, in and by the *ego*. Let this, therefore, be maintained: let the *fact* of the testimony be admitted, but the *truth* of the testimony, to aught beyond its own ideal existence, be doubted or denied. How in this case are we to proceed? It is evident that the doubt does not in this case refute itself. It is not suicidal by self-contradiction.

The *felo-de-se*, the very *suicide*, which Hamilton has always hitherto cast in the teeth of the cosmothetic idealist, is here formally, punctually retracted by Hamilton himself. Now then the cosmothetic idealist feels that justice has been done him at last, that his difficulty is at length fairly stated, that his question is here finally put just as he himself would wish to see it put. He may be forgiven, then, should he again allow himself to entertain the expectation of a tangible finding at last. As before, so here, however: the very next step, and his impatience begins; for Hamilton, instead of keeping by the thing now that he has come fairly up to it, instead of answering his own question, coolly looks off, turns aside to Stewart, from him again to Reid, then to Descartes, then to Cousin, enveloping himself all the while in a variety of quotations and remarks, till finally, the position lost to view by reason of the very number of the diversions, the only answer that comes out is, 'The doubt is gratuitous!'

'The deliverance of consciousness must philosophically be accepted,' so cries Hamilton for the thousandth time, and we are where we were—only that having, in this manner, been injured in the text, we find ourselves insulted in the notes thus:—

From what has now been stated [i.e. in the above passage] it will be seen how far and on what grounds I hold, at once with Dr. Reid and Mr. Stewart, that our original beliefs are to be established, but their authority not to be canvassed; and with M. Jouffroy, that the question of their authority is not to be absolutely withdrawn, as a forbidden problem, from philosophy.

Would or could any man that ever existed—but Hamilton—have written that note? Pray, observe—and as placed—its full significance and veritable bearing. Cannot we fancy the cosmothetic idealist ironically remarking to Hamilton:—Yes, I see, though true blue with Reid, you are liberal and candid with Jouffroy; the question is not withdrawn either;—*only*, when *my* mouth presumes to open on it, there comes a back-hander of veracious, veracious —here ferocious—that shuts it again: well, once I can speak for pain, I will tell you, Sir William, that it is a queer piece of *hedging, that* of holding both with Reid and with Jouffroy; and I cannot, somehow, feel quite certain that two *expressions* mean also always *two* things; for, if *allowed* by this word, I am *forbidden* by the other at all to question consciousness —unless under penalty of confounding and embroiling all?

While it is very clear, then, that Hamilton, at his *own* time, never scruples to allow himself the privilege of putting consciousness to the question, it is equally clear that he absolutely refuses at *any* time to share this privilege with that to him unclean animal—the cosmothetic idealist. Him he drives off ever with the fiercest refusals—the angriest denials. But, no more here than elsewhere, can Hamilton assert for himself what he denies for others—without *contradiction.* This, then, is still the burthen of the tale: wherever we move in Hamilton, there is always present to us the same element of inconsistency, discrepancy, and incongruity. Hence the fallacies; which here, too, are not wanting. It is probably quite impossible, for instance, to find anywhere a more striking example of 'artful diversion' than is furnished by the passage on which we have just commented. We may take the opportunity to remark, too, that an example of this same fallacy (the *ignoratio elenchi*), in the form of 'mistake' or 'misstatement,' was afforded by Hamilton's ascription to the Representationist in general, and Kant in particular, of regarding the representation (*Vorstellung*) perceived as, in any sense, a likeness or resemblance of the unknown antecedent. 'Imputed consequences,' again, or the remaining form of the *ignoratio elenchi*—this is the fallacy that pervades that elaborate description, now so familiar to us, of the results that follow the questioning of consciousness: our personality, our immortality, morality, society, religion, &c., &c. Strange that, with such a picture before him, sophistical though it be, Hamilton should still have so often admitted—if only for himself, indeed—the legitimacy of this very questioning—the legitimacy of transcending appearance, and of scientifically and systematically developing and evolving facts! The very lightness and ease with which he thus contradicts himself, now interdicting a single look into the adytum of consciousness, and again expressly exhorting us to approach, examine, and arrange, should alone be sufficient to demonstrate his own inward consciousness of the sandy and fallacious soil on which he had sought to build.

How different Hegel, to whom the antithesis is present also, but who sees not *only one side at a time*, like Hamilton, but always *both*! It is thus, that bringing *both* thoughts together, Hegel is able 'to transcend yet hold consciousness.' He, for his part, knows, too, that the vocation of philosophy is just to oppose—that with which Hamilton browbeats us—'the dogmatism of ordinary consciousness.' Philosophy, he says, 'begins by rising *over* common consciousness;' and (*Werke*, xvi. 108) with a reference that bears on what amounts to Hamilton's *loud* side—to his ὅτι, that is, or the inviolability of consciousness—he declares:—

Of this barbarism, to place undeniable certainty and verity in the facts of consciousness, neither ancient scepticism, nor any materialism, nor even the commonest common sense, unless an absolutely bestial one, has ever made itself guilty, —until the most recent times, it has been unheard of in philosophy.*

By consciousness here, we are of course to understand a consciousness, as it were, at first hand — a

---

* From this allusion in Hegel to the Hamiltonian cry of 'the veracity of consciousness,' and from other allusions in the same volume to other Hamiltonian cries or distinctions, as in reference to Idealism, Realism, &c., and as against an Absolute, we are led partly to see and partly to suspect that, in the works—and they are evidently *exoteric*—of Krug, Schulze, &c., Hegel had then a matter before him much like that which we, in the works of Hamilton, have now before us, and that thus, probably, this last, even in his most peculiar industry, has been, to some extent, anticipated.

consciousness that, from the platform of common sense, testifies to 'the natural conviction of mankind' in the independent externality of an actual non-ego. It is to the same consciousness that Hegel alludes when he says elsewhere:—'In place of demonstration, there come forward assertions and the recountments of what is ready-found in consciousness as facts, which is held the purer, the more uncritical it is.' By implication, then, there is also to Hegel a consciousness at second hand, which, critically purged, is the consciousness of trust. It will add one more inconsistency to the long catalogue of such, should we find Hamilton, too, to end in such a consciousness as he could only similarly describe. Meantime we conclude here by the simple dilemma to which the factual position has brought us.

It will not be denied, namely, that Hamilton, while he conceives the testimony of consciousness which we consider here to be in its nature *sensuous*, conceives it also to be in its validity *apodictic*. On the first head, we remind only that Hamilton claims for himself 'the natural conviction of mankind'—a conviction which, even were Hamilton disposed to forget that he had himself affirmed, '*The very things* which we perceive by the senses do really exist,' will be allowed to believe in the matter-of-fact and sensuous nature of the external reality, the non-ego.* On the second head, again, it is quite certain that Hamilton assigns to the cognition of this non-ego both the universality and the necessity of a first or ultimate principle.

* See also the first extract, pp. 80-81.

Now, we know that no distinction accentuated by Kant, has been received with greater approbation by Hamilton than that which discriminates between the apodictic and the contingent: what is *à priori* or native to the mind is apodictic, what is *à posteriori* or empirical (sensuous) is only contingent. While Hume, too, had this same principle before him when he distinguished between relations of ideas and matters of fact, Hamilton himself—with a certain triumph—has pointed it out in Leibnitz. The evolution of the dilemma, then, has now no difficulty. It is seen at once in the contradiction that would identify a matter of fact, on this hand, and an apodictic validity on the other; and may be expressed thus:—

The cognition in question (Hamilton's ὅτι) is either apodictic, or it is contingent; but if, on the one horn, it is apodictic, then it is no matter of fact; and if, on the other horn, it is contingent, then it is no necessary first principle. Hamilton's further proceedings, indeed, as we shall presently see, are not unillustrated by these alternatives.

3. *The Analysis of Philosophy; or, Hamilton's* διότι.

Sir William Hamilton has covered, we may say, quite nine-tenths of his canvas with the blinding and dazzling scarlet of his ὅτι; and for no other purpose, as the reader is led to suppose always, than to overbear any tint of a διότι. It is not uncharacteristic, then, that he should come, in the end, to a διότι himself. It appears that the ὅτι, after all, is insufficient, or that if 'every *how* rests ultimately on a *that*,' the *that* itself requires a more ultimate *how*. In this Hamilton defers to the natural longing for explanation, the instinct that turns unconsciously and by irresistible necessity in us to solution and resolution of every ὅτι into a διότι. For this, too, is the truth: if the *how* must rest on a *that*, the *that* must equally rest on a *how*. The ὅτι itself, indeed, is not more *that* than *because*. This, however, does not mitigate the contradiction that lies here again at the door of Hamilton, who really ought to have been less violent with his *that*, seeing that he was minded to follow so soon with his *how*. In fact, as we saw before, it is a *macula* in Hamilton that he should have been obliged to supplement the irrefragable consciousness he claimed by any analysis of philosophy at all—a *macula*, we may say, *squared* by the actual examples given of this botched analysis itself—and a *macula* raised, finally, even into an unknown degree by the consideration that, despite both the testimony of consciousness and the analysis of philosophy, the external realities themselves, that were, in the first instance, known in themselves and as they existed, were, in the second instance, *not* known in themselves and as they existed, but remained, at last, and for *all* instances, incomprehensible, incognisable, unknown, zero!

These are awkward preliminaries certainly ; still it is to be allowed that the analysis of philosophy may, after all, show much better in itself than in the examples we know it by; and this notwithstanding even that the cipher of the apparent result would bid us still despair. But, be this as it may, let us see now, in effect, how Hamilton actually has acquitted

himself of that evolution of the fact which, in honour
of the fact, he at first refused. This evolution, principally contained in the Dissertations to Reid, is the
Hamiltonian Theory of *Perception*—a word which
Hamilton now characteristically allows to reappear,
instead of the *consciousness* in which he formerly
sought to merge it.

We premise the following quotations:—

The developed doctrine of Real Presentationism, the basis
of Natural Realism, asserts the consciousness of immediate
perception of certain essential attributes of matter objectively
existing; while it admits that other properties of bodies are
unknown in themselves, and only inferred as causes to
account for certain subjective affections of which we are
cognisant in ourselves. (Reid's *Works*, p. 825.) I hold that,
though sensation proper be the condition of, and therefore
anterior to, perception proper in the order of nature, that, in
the order of time, both are necessarily co-existent;—the
latter being only realised in and through the present existence of the former. . . . Sensations of secondary qualities
imply an idiopathic affection of the nervous organism; but
such affection requires only the excitation of an appropriate stimulus; while such stimulus may be supplied by
manifold agents of the most opposite nature, both from
within the body and from without. . . . I hold that, on the
one hand, in the consciousness of sensations, out of each
other, contrasted, limited, and variously arranged, we have
a perception proper of the primary qualities, in an externality, though not to the nervous organism, as an immediate
cognition, and not merely as a notion or concept, of something extended, figured, &c.; and, on the other, as a correlative contained in the consciousness of our voluntary
motive energy resisted, and not resisted by aught within the
limits of mind and its subservient organs, we have a perception proper of the secundo-primary quality of resistance in
an extra-organic force, as an immediate cognition, and not

merely as a notion or concept, of a resisting something
external to our body:—though certainly in either case there
may be, and probably is, a concomitant act of imagination,
by which the whole complex consciousness on the occasion
is filled up. (Reid's *Works*, pp. 882-4.) The mind, when a
material existence is brought into relation with its organ of
sense, obtains two concomitant and immediate cognitions
. . . the one the secondary qualities of body; the other the
primary qualities of body. Of these cognitions, the former
is admitted, on all hands, to be subjective and ideal; the
latter, the Natural Realist maintains, against the Cosmothetic Idealist, to be objective and real. . . . The secondary
qualities, as mere sensations, mere consciousness of certain subjective affections, afford us no immediate knowledge of aught
different from self. (Reid's *Works*, p. 820.) The perception
proper, accompanying a sensation proper, is not an apprehension, far less a representation, of the external or internal
stimulus, or concause, which determines the affection whereof
the sensation is the consciousness. Not the former; for the
stimulus or concause of a sensation is always, in itself, to
consciousness unknown. Not the latter; for this would turn
perception into imagination—reduce it from an immediate
and assertory and objective, into a mediate and problematic
and subjective cognition. In this respect, perception proper
is an apprehension of the relations of sensations to each
other, primarily in space, and secondarily in time and degree.
(Reid's *Works*, p. 881.) In the primary, the sensation, the
condition of the perception, is not itself caused by the objective quality perceived; in the secundo-primary, the concomitant sensation is the effect of the objective quality
perceived; in the secondary, the sensation is the effect of
an objective quality supposed, but not perceived. (Reid's
Works, p. 860.) All the senses, simply or in combination,
afford conditions for the perception of the primary qualities,
and all, of course, supply the sensations themselves of the
secondary. As only various modifications of resistance, the
secundo-primary qualities are all, as percepts proper, as

quasi-primary qualities, apprehended through the locomotive
faculty, and our consciousness of its energy; as sensations,
as secondary qualities, they are apprehended as modifications
of touch proper, and of cutaneous and muscular feeling.
(Reid's *Works*, p. 864.) The secondary, as manifested to us,
are not, in propriety, qualities of body at all . . . they are
only subjective affections . . . of which alone we are immediately cognisant, the external concause of the internal effect
remaining to perception altogether unknown. (Reid's *Works*,
p. 854.) The more determinate senses are no less subjective
than the others. (Reid's *Works*, p. 855.) [And he passes in
review sight, hearing, &c., asserting of each and all that the
sensible affection may be excited by a variety of stimuli,
external and internal, ' that it does not cease with the presence, and, therefore, does not demonstrate the quality of
the external object.'] The secundo-primary qualities have
all relation to space, and motion in space; and are all contained under the category of resistance or pressure. On
their primary or objective phasis, they manifest themselves
as *degrees* of resistance opposed to our locomotive energy;
on their secondary or subjective phasis, as *modes* of resistance
or pressure affecting our sentient organism. (Reid's *Works*,
p. 848.) On space are dependent what are called the primary
qualities of body, and space combined with degree affords, of
body, the secundo-primary qualities. (*Disc.* p. 607.)

These extracts will make the various qualities
—primary, secondary, and secundo-primary—plain.
Evidently, too, any consideration that may decide
on the two former will equally decide on the last
as but a together of both. Now, as we soon learn,
a certain fine, free, easy ascent over Kant is one of
Hamilton's commonest grand airs. We have seen,
indeed, how, when requiring his testimony to relativity, he sweetly named him the philosopher of
Königsberg. This is by no means, however, his usual

tone. No; on the contrary, the ascent alluded to is generally effected in a mood of the loftiest censure, of the most gravely assumed reprobation. Nevertheless, it is quite plain from these extracts that, on his own showing, Hamilton, so far as he goes in perception, (or all reference to the categories apart), is not in any respect—at least, any respect that is not a mistake of his own—different from Kant. They are agreed, namely, on the fact of an external world. They are agreed on the secondary qualities, which are to both but states of our own dependent on unknown stimuli. They are agreed on the primary qualities,—both reducing them to space. And they are agreed lastly, as Hamilton also unequivocally declares, on space itself; so far, that is, as it is to both a native, necessary, and *à priori* cognition of the mind. Hamilton, however, preserves still his horror of the cosmothetic idealist—pushing him off, indeed, by the infinite breadth of a whole *real* space; but this concerns only the already mentioned mistake. In a word, Hamilton conceives Kant's space to be wholly inner, sees not that it is outer as well; and so, supervacaneously doubling it, adds on another unnecessary space of his own. Or Hamilton, accepting Kant's space, insists on botching it with an empirical side which it already abundantly possesses. An extract will explain :—

That the notion of space is a necessary condition of thought, and that, as such, it is impossible to derive it from experience, has been cogently demonstrated by Kant. But that we may not, through sense, have empirically an immediate perception of something extended, I have yet seen no valid reason to doubt. The *à priori* conception does not exclude the *à posteriori* perception. (Reid's *Works*, p. 126, note.) Our cognitions of extension and its modes are not wholly ideal; although space be a native, necessary, *à priori* form of imagination, and so far, therefore, a mere subjective state, there is, at the same time, competent to us, in an *immediate* perception of external things, the consciousness of a really existent, of a really objective extended world. (Reid's *Works*, p. 841.) The doctrine of Kant [with which Hamilton concurs]—that time is a fundamental condition, form, or category of thought. (Reid's *Works*, p. 124, note.) On this principle [Necessity], as first evolved,—at least, first signalised by Kant, *space* and *time* are merely modifications of mind. (*Disc.* p. 273.) [See also Reid's *Works*, pp. 343, 847, and *Meta.* i. 403 ; ii. 114, 166–170.]

Now, it is quite certain that Kant would not have rejected these expressions of Hamilton in regard to our having through sense an empirical perception of something extended, of a really objective extended world, &c. To Kant, as little as to Hamilton, were our cognitions of extension wholly ideal; and no more to the latter than to the former did the *à priori* conception exclude the *à posteriori* perception.

We are not left any room to doubt, then, of the state of Hamilton's mind in reference to the mentioned doctrines of Kant. Conceptively, he accepts them: perceptively, he—not rejects them—but knows them not. Hamilton, in fact, has never dreamed that the time and space of Kant are *perceptive* and not—we may, indeed, say this—conceptive. To him, time as understood by Kant is only 'a condition, form, or category of *thought* ;' space, similarly, is only 'a condition of *thought*,' 'a form of *imagination*,' 'an *à priori* conception, not an *à posteriori* perception.' He, for his part, and as, in his own idea, opposed to Kant, holds that 'space and time, as given, are real forms of thought and—*conditions of things*' (*Meta.* i. 403); and (same page), he says of Kant: 'if he does not deny, he will not affirm the existence of a real space external to our minds.' It is in a similar frame of mind that, referring to Kant as holding the subjective nature of space, he adds, 'but in this he varies,'— meaning, evidently, that he knows of Kant speaking at times as if he held space to be objectively existent. Now, if he had not insinuated, but openly announced this, he would only have stated the truth. Kant, in fact, *always* says this, and varies *never*.

In short, Hamilton knows only the subjective, intellectual, and conceptive side of Kant's space and time; he knows only one side, he knows not the other; he knows not that these intellectual, *à priori* forms are, in actual, empirical fact, sensuously or *à posteriori* presentant;—he knows not that there is a provision in the theory of Kant whereby they become externalised, materialised, realised, or, as Hamilton might say, objectivised — though their veritable source and seat be subjective, ideal, internal, all the same. It is from this misconception and mistake that he finds Kant to 'vary,' and that he can come to say of him, 'if he does not deny, he will not affirm,' &c.

But this side existing in the theory of Kant, Hamilton's supposed complement is perceived at once to be neutralised and negated even by its own excess; and for excision of the excrescence, Kant himself (quite as much as, and in priority to, Hamilton) will extend to us the law of parsimony—Occam's razor!

But this side *does* exist in the theory of Kant. We are not called upon to demonstrate here: it is sufficient to indicate. Kant's time and space are of this nature, then, that, ideal, perceptive forms, native to the mind—sensuous spectra, optical discs—they, on hint of the stimuli of special sense, present themselves to the mind by or through special sense, as external recipients in which these stimuli (or their effects) dispose themselves before us in such manner that the peculiarity of their arrangement in space and time is due to their own secret nature, at the same time that the general fields of space and time are really furnished to them by the mind itself.

There is no occasion, then, to burthen such a space and time with the superfluity of Hamilton's addition. The empirical side which is all that that addition proposes to extend to them—this they already possess in themselves; and Hamilton would never have thought of it, had he at all seen the true scope of the theory. Not only, then, has Hamilton perpetrated a glaring blunder in respect to Kant, not only has he with a most redundant prodigality carried coals to a Newcastle already filled, but he has done worse: he has exposed himself to the edge of Occam's razor, and not only in that respect but also in this, that he has granted Kant's doctrine to be a demonstrated doctrine, and yet has generously given it in gift the very articles it supposed itself to have abolished and supplanted! Why—in the name of all parsimony, in the name of all rational economy!—should time and space have been laboriously built into the mind (as Hamilton admits), if (as Hamilton adds) they were there on the outside, actual objects, for the apprehension of which we possessed our own special five senses?

Had Hamilton, indeed, been duly awake here, he would have seen at once that Kant's *reine Anschauung*, possessing no matter but these *à priori* sensuous forms of space and time, was, feature for feature, identical with his own perception proper, possessing no matter but those primary qualities which he himself acknowledged to derive from—to be but modes of, space and time. Nay, duly awake, he would have perceived that Kant, not only in *naming* these forms perceptions (and as against conceptions), but in *proving* them perceptions (and as against conceptions), actually contemplated their empirical use, or as Hamilton might say, their objective presentation,—and this, their necessary, mental, *à priori* nature notwithstanding. But to have perceived this—and in a demonstrated doctrine—would have been to have perceived also the supererogatoriness of his own addition. The *eyes* to a *reality* of *actual outer* space which he desiderated in the doctrine of Kant, that doctrine already abundantly possessed; and his own proffered surgery, therefore, was obviously quite uncalled for. In short, the complement of Hamilton is refuted by a *reductio ad absurdum*.

But, in confutation of Hamilton, we are not limited to his resolution, on the one hand, of his primary qualities into space; and to his adoption, on the other,

of space itself as shown to be constituted by Kant;—
we can readily accomplish the same result by a consideration of these primary qualities themselves. For
this purpose, we supplement the quotations already
made by a few others, and in the more restricted
reference:—

Aristotle enumerates five *percepts* common to all or to a
plurality of the senses,—viz.: Magnitude (extension), figure,
motion, rest, number; but virtually admits, that these (the
common) are abusively termed *sensibles* at all, and are (in
one place he even says they are only apprehended *per accidens*), in fact, within the domain of sense, merely as being
the concomitants, or consequents (ἀκολουθοῦντα, ἑπομένα) of
the proper.... St. Thomas, showing that the common sensibles
do not, primarily and of themselves, act upon and affect the
sense, carries them all up into modifications of quantity....
Sensibilia communia omnia pertinent aliquo modo ad *continuum*. ... The several common sensibles are in reality
apprehended by other and higher energies than those of sense
... are not so much perceptions of sense (in so far as sensible
perception depends on corporeal affection) as concomitant
cognitions to which the impression on the organ by the
proper sensible only affords the occasion. (Reid's *Works*,
pp. 828–830.) [Kant's time and space can be characterised by
precisely the same words. Hutcheson holds that] extension, figure, motion, and rest seem to be more properly
ideas accompanying the sensations of sight and touch than
the sensations of either of these senses. (Reid's *Works*, pp. 124,
829.) [Reid himself says], upon the whole, it appears that
our philosophers have imposed upon themselves and upon us
in pretending to deduce from sensation the first origin of our
notions of external existences, of space, motion, and extension, and all the primary qualities of body—that is, the
qualities whereof we have the most clear and distinct conception ... they have no resemblance to any sensation, or to any
operation of our minds; and, therefore, they cannot be ideas

either of sensation or of reflection [no, says Kant, they attach to the sensuous, but *à priori*, spectra, space and time]. (Reid's *Works*, p. 126.) The primary qualities of matter thus develop themselves with rigid necessity out of the simple *datum*—substance occupying space. In a certain sort, and by contrast to the others, they are, therefore, notions, *à priori*, and to be viewed, *pro tanto*, as products of the understanding. (Reid's *Works*, p. 848.) [The apprehension of the primary qualities is called] purely spiritual [and they themselves] necessary and universal. (Reid's *Works*, pp. 858, 865: see also the description of the primary qualities in the previous quotation, Reid's *Works*, p. 860.)

These extracts—and many others might be added to the same effect—we may allowably assume to be sufficient in themselves. The general tenour of them, indeed, goes to show that the primary qualities are not cognitions of sense at all, but result from an intellectual, spiritual, spontaneous energy of the mind itself. In short, the entire relative argumentation of Hamilton unequivocally demonstrates the necessary, *à priori*, and so *mental* nature of all his own percepts proper. It is quite certain, nevertheless, that Hamilton does attach a sensuous nature to these percepts all the same, and what we would point out is, that Hamilton, on his own principles, ought to have seen into the preposterousness of this addition, both in their case individually, and in that of space as their matrix in general. Hamilton is perfectly aware that the signs which separate the pure or *à priori* from the empirical or *à posteriori* are necessity and universality. We find him again and again stating this: we find him, indeed, with an *allure* customary to him, quoting Leibnitz on this point with a view to lessen the relative merit of Kant. Leibnitz, he says, remarks that 'the senses indeed inform us what may take place, but not what necessarily takes place,' &c. (*Meta.* ii. 347.) In truth, with this criterion of necessity so distinctly present to his mind, and in view of the issues so markedly emerging from the theory of Kant, it is surprising that Hamilton should have attempted a task so self-contradictory and absurd as an induction from experience of matters that plainly preceded, and were independent of, all experience; but it is still more surprising that, of Kant's four reasons as regards the nature of space, two of them were advanced directly to prove that space was a *perception* and not a *conception*, and that Hamilton should not have known as much.*

Hamilton, then, pronouncing his own percepts proper, or the primary qualities, to hold of the understanding rather than of sense, and ascribing to them, moreover, the peculiar necessity and validity we signalise, ought to have seen that, as they were impossibly contingent or *à posteriori*, they must be *à priori*, and not empirical at all. His error with these, in fact, is identical with his error with space: he failed to perceive that, though mental, they might, by projection, pass into the contingent, and return with the contingent for actual apprehension by special sense;—not, however, that they themselves, or any element of

---

* This is a clear proof that Hamilton was indebted for the very imperfect little he knew of Kant to the ' literature of the subject.' It is also a clear proof of the precarious nature of book-manipulation, even with the very quickest eye; for few things are more *eye-catching* in Kant than his formal arguments in reference to space. But see ii. 2.

them, had any source whatever but the mind itself. It is particularly interesting, indeed, to collate the difficulties of Aristotle and the rest with the focal solution into which Kant, almost by their own arguments, finally reduced them.

Apart, then, this untenable sensuous side, which, however, we shall presently examine for itself, it is impossible any longer for Hamilton to refuse the companionship of Kant—it is impossible any longer for Hamilton to refuse the title of cosmothetic idealist. He himself points to the primary qualities as the only septum that in his own belief exists to separate him from Kant. These primary qualities he himself resolves into space, and space itself he accepts at the hands of Kant. There is nothing, then, between them but an unnecessary *real* space due to his own mistake; and, this mistake corrected, septum there is none, the drops have coalesced, they are now one: Hamilton, already so largely relativist and phenomenalist, is now wholly such, and the discussion is finished.

This sensuous side of Hamilton constitutes, however, perhaps the very most interesting element in the whole of his industry, and cannot be passed over. It is an element, indeed, that, whether in that he read, or whether in that he thought, may be almost named his centre. The following extracts will, with those that precede, elucidate our meaning :—

This extreme doctrine [alluding to that referred to in the quotations above from Aristotle, the Schoolmen, Hutcheson, Reid, &c.] is not, however, to be admitted. As sensibles, the common [i. e., the percepts proper, the primary qualities] must be allowed to act somehow upon the sense, though in a different manner from the proper. Comparatively speaking, the proper act primarily, corporeally, and by causing a passion in the sense; the common secondarily, formally, and by eliciting the sense and understanding to energy. But though there lies in the proper more of passivity, in the common more of activity, still the common are, in propriety, objects of sense per se; being neither cognised (as substances) exclusively by the understanding, nor (as is the sweet by vision) accidentally by sense. (Reid's *Works*, p. 860.) [Here, evidently, it is not *fact* that prescribes so and so; but just Hamilton that, for his own convenience, says so and so: the common sensibles are held or demonstrated to be intellectual, but I, Hamilton, *will* them to be also sensuous, and accordingly they *are* also sensuous. It is this wilfulness, however, that has impaled Hamilton on the horns of the dilemma with which the preceding sub-section (2) ends.]

It may appear, not a paradox merely, but a contradiction, to say, that the organism is, at once, within and without the mind; is at once subjective and objective; is at once ego and non-ego. But so it is; the organism, as animated, as sentient, is necessarily ours, and its affections are only felt as affections of the individual ego. In this respect, and to this extent, our organs are not external to ourselves. But our organism is not merely a sentient subject, it is at the same time an extended, figured, divisible, in a word, a material, subject; and the same sensations, which are reduced to unity in the indivisibility of consciousness, are in the divisible organism recognised as plural and reciprocally external, and, therefore, as extended, figured, divided. (Reid's *Works*, p. 880, note.)

By a law of our nature, we are not conscious of the existence of our organism (as a body simply), consequently not conscious of any of its primary qualities, unless when we are conscious of it, as modified by a secondary quality, or some other of its affections, as an animated body. But the former consciousness requires the latter only as its negative condition, and is neither involved in it as a part, nor properly dependent on it as a cause. The object in the one consciousness is also wholly different from the object in the other. In *that*, it is a contingent passion of the organism, as a constituent of the human self; in *this*, it is some essential property of the organism, as a portion of the universe of matter, and though apprehended by, not an affection proper to, the conscious self at all. In these circumstances, the secondary quality, say a colour, which the mind apprehends in the organism, is, as a passion of self, recognised to be a *subjective object*; whereas the primary quality, extension, or figure, or number, which, when conscious of such affection, the mind therein at the same time apprehends, is, as not a passion of self, but a common property of matter, recognised to be an *objective object*. (Reid's *Works*, p. 858, note.)

It is sufficient to establish the simple fact, that we are competent, as consciousness assures us, immediately to apprehend through sense the non-ego in certain limited relations; and it is of no consequence whatever, either to our certainty of the reality of a material world, or to our ultimate knowledge of its properties, whether by this primary apprehension we lay hold, in the first instance, on a larger or a lesser portion of its contents. (Reid's *Works*, p. 814.) The perception of parts out of parts is not given in the mere affection of colour, but is obtained by a reaction of the mind upon such affection. The secondary quality of colour is, in the strictest sense, a passive affection of the sentient ego. . . . But the apprehension of extension, figure, divisibility, &c., which, under condition of its being thus affected, simultaneously takes place, is, though necessary, wholly active and purely spiritual. (Reid's *Works*, p. 858.) [Thus an] Error of the common opinion, that the apprehension through sight of colour, and the apprehension through sight of extension and figure, are as inseparable, identical cognitions of identical objects. (Reid's *Works*, p. 860.) The observations of Platner, on a person born blind, would prove that *sight*, not *touch*, is the sense by which we principally obtain our knowledge of figure, and our *empirical* knowledge of space. (Reid's *Works*, p. 125, note.) It is self-evident that, if a thing is to be an object *immediately* known, it must be known as it exists. Now, a body must exist in some definite part of space—in a certain *place*; it cannot, therefore, be immediately known *as existing*, except it be known *in its place*. But this supposes the mind to be immediately present to it in space. (Reid's *Works*, p. 302, note.) We are not percipient of distant objects. (Reid's *Works*, p. 814.) No sense gives us a knowledge of aught but what is *in immediate contact* with its organ. All else is something over and above perception . . . and only reached by reasoning. (Reid's *Works*, p. 145, note; 186, note.) The total object of visual perception is the rays and the living organ in reciprocity. (Reid's *Works*, p. 160, note.)

The object of consciousness in perception is a quality, mode, or phenomenon *of an external reality*, in immediate relation to our organs. (Reid's *Works*, p. 818.) A sensation is actually felt there where it is felt to be . . . in the toe, not in the brain. . . . If the mind be conscious of the secondary qualities only at the centre, it cannot be conscious of the primary in their relation to its periphery. (Reid's *Works*, p. 821. See also p. 882, as quoted previously.) Perception proper is an apprehension of the relations of sensations to each other, primarily in space. (p. 881.) In the consciousness of sensations, relatively localised and reciprocally external, we have a veritable apprehension and consequently an immediate perception, of the affected organism as extended, divided, figured, &c. (p. 884.) Extension is perceived only in apprehending sensations out of sensations—a relation. . . . The only object perceived is the organ itself, as modified, or what is in contact with the organ as resisting. The doctrine of a medium is an error. (p. 885.) The mind perceives nothing external to itself, except the affections of the organism as animated, the reciprocal relations of these affections, and the correlative involved in the consciousness of its locomotive energy being resisted. (p. 885.) [From the quotation previously given (p. 860) we see that the object of the *sensation* is not the object of the *perception*.]

That through touch, or touch and muscular feeling, or touch and sight, or touch, muscular feeling, and sight,—that through these senses exclusively, we are percipient of extension, &c., I do not admit. On the contrary, I hold that all sensations whatsoever, of which we are conscious, as one out of another, *eo ipso*, afford us the condition of immediately and necessarily apprehending extension; for in the consciousness itself of such reciprocal outness is actually involved a perception of difference of place in space, and, consequently, of the extended. (p. 861.)

[At p. 876 (Reid's *Works*) his general doctrine is pretty well stated at full. He enumerates there *eight* conditions of consciousness and perception. These are, shortly: 1, Attention; 2, discriminated plurality, alteration, difference in objects themselves (with contrast of object and subject); 3, quality; 4, time, involving memory; 5, space, as condition of a discriminated plurality; 6, degree; 7, relation; 8, an assertory judgment, &c.]

The primary qualities are perceived as in our organism. ... Thus a perception of the primary qualities does not, originally and in itself, reveal to us the existence, and qualitative existence, of aught beyond the organism, apprehended by us as extended, figured, divided, &c. ... The primary qualities of things external to our organism we do not perceive, i. e. *immediately know*. For these we only learn to *infer*. ... This experience [on which knowledge of the external world depends] presupposes, indeed, a notion of space and motion in space. ... On the doctrine, and in the language, of Reid, our original cognitions of space, motion, &c., are instinctive; a view which is confirmed by the analogy of those of the lower animals which have the power of locomotion at birth. It is truly an idle problem to attempt imagining the steps by which we may be supposed to have acquired the notion of extension; when, in fact, we are unable to imagine to ourselves the possibility of that notion not being always in our possession. [But still he decides] We have, therefore, a twofold cognition of space; *a*, an *à priori, native* imagination of it in general, as a necessary condition of the possibility of thought; and *b*, under that an *à posteriori* or adventitious percept of it, &c. (p. 881.)

Though the sensation of our organism as animally affected, is, as it were, the light by which it is exhibited to our perception as a physically extended body; still, if the affection be too strong, the pain or pleasure too intense, the light blinds by its very splendour, and the perception is lost in the sensation. (pp. 862–3.)

The ultimate fibrils are the ultimate units of sensation ... a nervous point yields a sensation as locally distinct in proportion as it is isolated in its action from every other. (p. 862.) On the smaller size of the papillæ and fibrils of the optic nerve, principally depends the greater power we possess, in the eye, of discriminating one sensation as out of another, consequently of apprehending extension, figure, &c.

[At p. 821, as we saw, Hamilton rules that to restrict the mind to the centre, and exclude it from the periphery, is equivalent to representationism. Now, in a note to p. 861, he withdraws this, and rules that the mind may be confined to the centre without injury to his theory—each nervous filament, however long, may be still viewed as a point. In presence of the decisive distinctness *here*, we think of the punctual peremptoriness *there*; and when Hamilton lightly remarks, 'what was said at p. 821 is to be qualified in conformity,' we consider the contrariety, the lightness, the *aplomb* as all three eminently characteristic.] The diameter of the papillæ of the optic nerve is about the eight or nine thousandth part of an inch; ... and a stimulus of light, though applied only to part of a papilla, idiopathically affects the whole; ... an object, whose breadth, as reflected to the retina, is not more than the six hundred thousandth or millionth of an inch, is distinctly visible to a good eye. (p. 862.) [Distinction in touch he attributes to the isolated fibrils—where distinction is impossible to touch, he is sure that there microscopic anatomy will find an interlacement of fibrils, or an expansion of one.—p. 863.]

Hamilton's theory lies—pretty well completely—in these extracts; and, using an illustration, it is shortly this:—The mind inhabits a certain vase, and so that it is directly present to every unit of the extension of this vase. But, single unit or entire extension, these are quite unknown to it *till lit*. Lit, however, the entire vase is exhibited to it (the mind) with the constituent units of the vase relatively localised and reciprocally out of one another, as extension implies. Further, now, this vase moves; and, moving, is resisted. If before, then, the vase itself gave knowledge of a partly outer and a partly inner, resistance gives knowledge now of a wholly outer. To this wholly outer, the facts learned of the partly outer are next inferentially transferred. Lastly, the light that lit the partly outer, is also inferentially transferred to this same wholly outer as to its cause. In this way it is, that, to Hamilton's belief, the knowledge of the external world is constituted.*

Of this theory the mind's net, the nervous envelope, the organism, or, rather we may say at once, the ocular membrane, is the centre of gravity. Reference to the quotations generally, and especially to that from Reid's *Works*, pp. 862–3, will readily decide this. In short, throughout the entire theory, it is the *lit ocular membrane* that is present to Hamilton's thought. This membrane affected, a light is struck in it, and the threads of its extension seen. Or, in the light of the secondary quality, the mind perceives the extension

---

* See the last paragraph of the quotations for a point in the above where Hamilton vacillates.

of the primary quality. 'The passion of colour first
rising into consciousness, not from the amount of the
intensive quantity of the affection, but from the
amount of the extensive quantity of the organism
affected, is necessarily apprehended under the condition of extension.' (Reid's *Works*, p. 885.) Each ultimate fibril of the membrane is a lit point, and these lit
points are relatively localised and reciprocally external.
The light, as it were, carries these points into the mind
which cognises them, consequently, as they are thus
mutually *in situ*. However small the ocular membrane, any amount of an externality actually known
is enough: all the rest follows easily *on* resistance—*to*
transference—*through* inference.

Hamilton, then, evidently, presupposes mind, body,
and outer world; and the only question to him is,
How does the first come to know the second and the
third? The netted mind is further netted: how does
it come to perceive its own net, and its net's net? The
latter Hamilton does not conceive to be '*perceived*,' to
be 'immediately known' at all. It is certainly a place
of knowledge, but there is nothing known in it that
is not the result of inference and transference referred
to the former. It is in the mind's net, then, that all
that is important to Hamilton occurs; and this is
neither complicated nor hard to conceive. The mind,
already present to the net, is, by sensation in the net,
as it were, *fired* to perception of the net. This is the
whole—there is, indeed, no more than this; for resistance itself only adopts this for simple externalisation
one step further. That is to say, the nervous net

being flushed, coloured, or lit by a sensation, or secondary quality, there is perception of this net itself in its primary qualities. This is the ultimate fact—the ultimate *that* (ὅτι). On sense of resistance then, again, these primary qualities of the nervous net (together with the secondary of the same) are transferred to an unknown substrate that resists; and so by continued process of inference there gradually rises around us the formed world.

The mind, then, to Hamilton, though pervading the nervous net that envelops it, perceives this net only when it (the net) is lit by a secondary quality; and even then, be it remembered, not in itself—no, only in its modes, which modes are the primary qualities. These primary qualities—modes of a non-ego; for the nervous net, if on one side within the mind, is on another side without the mind, and in that aspect other than the mind—are transferred by inference to the non-ego beyond the nervous net; what we called the net's net; which ulterior non-ego, or net, is itself inferred on occasion of *resistance* to the voluntary locomotion of the netted mind.* Thus is it that

---

* Hamilton certainly figures sensation of secondary and perception of primary quality (though impossibly else than a sequence of first and second both in nature and in time—though quite as much so, indeed, as any sequence of two terms that can be anywhere referred to), as a single organic act; and it is very possible that he would wish to associate with these, and in this act, the element of resistance as well. Such association, at least, might, perhaps, relieve the difficulty as to when and where Hamilton places the first cognition of outness; for cognition of a non-ego that is at once within the mind and without the mind, seems competent rather to *otherness* than to *outness*. *Thorough* outness is, perhaps, hardly possible *before* resistance. This difficulty, however, probably never occurred to Hamilton.

Hamilton conceives the mind to arrive at cognition of its entire abode. All knowledge of outer things is but an *inferential transference* from the *netted mind* to *resistants* without. These resistants without, again, are unknown things in themselves actually presented to the netted mind; but they are also only phenomena, in that they are not known in themselves, but only through, first, the primary qualities transferred, so to speak, *in* to their interiors, and, second, the secondary qualities inferentially transferred *on* to their exteriors. The former inference, again, to Hamilton, is presentative or noumenal in its validity, while the latter is only representative or phenomenal: that is to say, the resistants he conceives to *possess* the primary qualities; but they are not, by any means, *necessarily* even the causes, excitants, or stimuli of the very secondary qualities which by inference of the mind are, as their effects, reflected to them.

Hamilton thus conceives himself surrounded by unknown resistants which, substantiated by the primary qualities and clothed by the secondary, open up into, or rather simply take on, this coloured and variegated universe; and we may now more clearly realise to ourselves the precise burthen and bearing of his presentative phenomenalism, or of his presented phenomenon. Cognition, as only relative (which is simply a matter of course to Hamilton), *must* be phenomenal, but to this cognition the phenomenon concerned is an actually present other, or to this cognition an external something is actually *there*, under whatever amount of phenomenal shimmer. A hat may, by design, by accident, by age, take on this shape, that shape, and a hundred shapes; this colour, that colour, and a hundred colours; but, under every shape, and under every colour (or however phenomenally varied), it may conceivably retain the same substance, and remain the same non-ego, or hat, still. Each of the surrounding, unknown substrates, then, is but such presented phenomenon; noumenal knowledge does not exist—even the primary qualities are relative and modified modes (Hamilton's own language); nevertheless, knowledge is not confined to one's own self, to one's own states—it really concerns a non-ego, or non-egos, actually presented. There *are* outer things that, though unknown in themselves, hold up, through force of the primary qualities, all the variegated colouring of the secondary. Hamilton evidently cannot do without the supporting frames and skeletons of these outer substrates; they are to him what the *Anstoss* was to Fichte, the plane and planes of reflexion from which there return to the ego—but now as outer and other—the ego's own states (the secondary qualities). An *outer* kernel of support plays a *rôle* indispensable to Hamilton, and he can see for it no substitute, no surrogate, anywhere else. Had Hamilton, it is true, as we have seen, but understood the relative doctrine, he might have found this substitute, this surrogate, in the space of Kant, in which his own primary qualities are admittedly implied. Had projection, indeed, from within out, of such a spectrum as Kant's space, occurred to Hamilton, he would probably not have hesitated to adopt the simpler, the more comprehensive, the more adequate, the more consistent, and the more satisfactory theory. To declare the primary qualities (space) his own state, did not for Kant dispossess these of the advantage they might offer as outer supports. They really, by reflexion, stood around him without, and thus really performed for the secondary qualities the very same function that Hamilton desiderated in his own unknown substrates.

Certainly the theory is exceedingly ingenious, but it is subjected, at the same time, to a variety of very serious objections. Must we not say, for example, that it is, after all, a beginning at the wrong end? If we are allowed to start at once as accomplished physiologists with the whole anatomy of the nervous system before us, have we not an easy game from the first? And as to that, indeed, are there not always too many physiological elements present to suit interests which concern psychology alone? Had Hamilton *deduced* his materials, physiological elements included, from any necessary and demonstrated basis, as is now always the indispensable preliminary of philosophy, both objections would fall; but such *deduction* fails. Then the direct presence of the mind to its own nervous organism must be regarded as a gratuitous assumption, unsupported by proof, and unillustrated by consciousness.

But, supposing this, how is it that the mind is not at once conscious of that which, *ex hypothesi*, it is directly present to? This would be immediate knowledge, and it is immediate knowledge which Hamilton would establish. Instead of this, how is it that the mind, to reach the knowledge in question, has still to wait for the addition of yet another element, which would seem rather thus to *mediate* knowledge?

The problem is, How can the mind know an external object? The first answer is, We have senses by which to smell it, taste it, touch it, hear it, and see it. Yes, is the rejoinder; but analysis and consideration will demonstrate that sense in each of these five modes is adequate to no more than the excitation in the mind of a passion, affection, or subjective feeling, which—as in the mind, and occupying the mind, and, so to speak, colouring the mind in a manner nowise distinguishable from that in which a variety of confessedly internal elements, grief, joy, hate, &c., is capable of occupying and, so to speak, colouring the mind—is evidence of its own self, and for its own self, but not possibly of or for anything else beside. A sensation is only intensive,—it is only a passion; the mind, for the time, is this passion, and this passion is it : there is no hint in it of anything but itself,—there is not the slightest suggestion in it of any transition whatever. Give the mind light only —it fills it, the mind is it, and it is the mind; but what else is there, or what else can it suggest? Give the mind sound only,—is it conceivable that the mind could disjoin it from itself, any more than it could disjoin from itself anger, or hope, or fear? And as it is with these senses (sight and hearing), so also is it with the others. But if it be so with each singly, so also must it be with all together; for no addition of subjective to subjective can ever make an objective—

no addition of internal to internal can ever thicken into an external.

It is here, however, that Hamilton suggests, The mind does not and cannot perceive anything external to itself; but it becomes aware of *its own sentient organism* on condition of a colour, or a vibration (say), being excited in that organism by one, or other, or all, of the stated five modes; and the remaining world of cognition is thereafter built up by process of experiment, inference, and reasoning. To Hamilton, then, it appears that, though it might be difficult to understand how the mind, with no production before it but a subjective colouring of its own, should be able to perceive outer objects, no such difficulty would exist if the perception concerned, not outer objects, but the nervous system. But it is easy to see that if the nervous system have the advantage of *nearness* over the outer objects understood here, it is still, even as much as they, an *other*, an outer; and so, consequently, still separated from the mind, like them, by the whole diameter of being. Nearness in such circumstances is but as the grain of sand that is removed from the mountain while the surveyor measures it. In relation to the nervous system, the subjective affection is no more than it is in relation to other outer objects; and that *it* is known is intelligible, for it is evidence for itself; but that anything else because of it can—without any further evidence—be added as known, is unintelligible. Let the vibration—to call by that name each of the five respective affections—be A; we acknowledge that we know A; but is that any reason that we should be credited with a knowledge of B as well? A, the *sensation*, is evidence for A; but the *perception* B is a new act, and in its nature very different from, nay, the reverse of, A, and we have still a right to ask, Where is the evidence for this new act B, and how was it performed, or how was its information attained to? To say the mind *perceived* B because it *felt* A, is only to *say*; it is not to reason.

But Hamilton would have said, perhaps, A and B, as referring to the same sentient organism, are in reality identical and not different; the subjective sensation and the objective perception coincide and coinhere in the same identical unit. Yes, we may rejoin, but, when the mind acknowledges that unit as under sensation, it is present to it as to its self; whereas, when the mind acknowledges that unit as under perception, it is absent from it as from its not-self (for to have *distinguished* it as not-self is equivalent to such estrangement), and the cleft remains as impassable as ever. We acknowledge arrival at the hither side of this cleft—we acknowledge experience of the subjective moment; but we cannot see that arrival at the hither, is equivalent to arrival also at the further side, or that the subjective moment is identical with the objective. There are the *two* terms still—and *apart* still: what we want is *nexus* and *connexus*; and we want it as much as ever. There is no secondary quality—no sensation—other to Hamilton himself than a mere subjective feeling, and a subjective feeling takes no further than itself. That the mind should undergo

passions—passion after passion—this is conceivable;
but how there should add itself to this passion any
nisus on the part of the mind to sally out and cognise
its own nervous organism as extended, divided, &c.—
or how it should require this passion, and be unable to
sally out without this passion—this is inconceivable.
Nay, this passion itself is really in the mind; it is
not in the tissue, and any question of the tissue would,
so far, seem not to have any place. But let us say,
that, in the passion, the mind absorbs into itself the
nervous net as *its* and *it*; how is it then that it (the
mind) is immediately forced, by perception, to reject
this same net from itself as neither *its* nor *it*, but an
other, a non-ego? Knowing the sentient organism as
the ego, that we should be enabled, so contrariously,
to know it as the non-ego, or accepting it in the
sensation as A, that we should reject it, at the same
time, in the perception as B—it is this recoil of mind
back from matter on to itself, or it is this reflexion
from mind to matter—this transmutation of non-ego
into ego, and again of ego into non-ego—it is this, so
to speak, presto-trick that constitutes the difficulty;
and, if Hamilton seems to simplify it by moving the
two terms nearer each other, he in reality only complicates it by the introduction of a *third*—a third
which only adds its own difficulty, and demands a
new explanation of its own.

But Hamilton's favourite sense is sight, and his
illustration by predilection light. As we saw on
page 85, he considers the *sensation* the light by which
the nervous organism is 'exhibited' in *perception*;

and the figure, if very luminous so far as the general doctrine is concerned, needs only to be looked at to show, on the question of inner rationale, quite as unsatisfactory as any that might be borrowed from any other sense. The mind, for example, Hamilton would seem to think, though already pervading the membrane of the eye, is quite *blind* to this membrane till this membrane is lit. When lit, however, the mind, instantly confessing this membrane to be itself, experiences the sensation (colour, &c.); but, as instantly denying this membrane to be itself, it experiences the perception of an extended and divided non-ego. But do not the difficulties remain thus—of how the light exhibits, how the attention is excited, and how the one or the other should be at all necessary? It is simple information that we cannot see in the dark; but what is the meaning of the *mind* requiring light to see its net by?—what power can light have added to such an energy as the mind *there*? Nay, one would think that the mind, occupying the same position in both cases, would be less likely to attend to its net when filled and occupied (with light), than when empty and disengaged. Hamilton only doubles the apparatus. As it is to common belief, we have an eye whereby to see things; but as it is to Hamilton, we have an eye whereby to see the eye. Or Hamilton actually postulates an eye behind the eye—not only an eye of the body, but an eye of the mind; excess of light too, it would seem, being not more dazzling and perplexing to the one, than it is dazzling and perplexing to the other.

Though it is certainly the coloured or lighted ocular membrane that dominates Hamilton, he as certainly, so far as words go, attributes a like function to the other organs of sense. 'All the senses,' he says (Reid's *Works*, p. 864), 'simply or in combination, afford conditions for the perception of the primary qualities.' Let us for a moment, then, consider the other senses, and see if it be with them, as the illustration would, at least to a certain extent, appear to make it with sight. How is it with smell? On sensation of an odour, does the mind wake up to peruse its Schneiderian membrane? Or taste? On sensation of sapidity, does the mind re-act on, or is it reflected to, the amount of the palate affected by the sapid particles, and as divided and figured by their varying sapidity? Or hearing? On sensation of sound, does the mind, by instant rebound, stand at once by the wall of its own tympanum, objectively cognising the same? Obviously, there is no evidence for any assertion of the affirmative in either of these cases! In touch, again, is it to the skin, and the amount of skin covered, that the sensation proper of smoothness, or of roughness, wetness, dryness, warmness, coldness, directs the mind? Is it not proved by Hamilton himself that touch is a very bungler at guessing the size of the impressing body—a very bungler at extension? Then is not sight too, according to the same authority, but a form of touch? Do we know aught but 'the rays and the living organ in reciprocity?' The rays touch, then, and we have the subjective feeling light; but why should the mind revert to the organ on hint of this sort of touch, rather than on that of any other touch, and in any other organ? Is not the whole fancy of the mind seeing its eye because it is lit—is not the whole metaphor of light but a will-of-the-wisp to the self-complacent Hamilton?

So far, then, as the sensation proper is the condition of the perception proper, we cannot say that Hamilton has, in any way, assisted us beyond the *fact*: we see neither the necessity nor the modus operandi of the same. Hamilton, indeed, says as much as this himself, for the sensation is to him nexus and it is not nexus, it is necessary and it is not necessary, and evidently at last he has simply blindly settled himself into the *analogy of light*. Why any such stimulus is,—how it acts,—what it does,—Hamilton, taking up his position in the nervous system, is even worse off for an answer here than common sense, which, unlike its professing votary, has really its seat on the ground. It is easy, in the straits of such questions, to bawl out ὅτι, and threaten us with a charge of imbecility at the hands of Aristotle; but, in the end, is there a single difficulty removed? Can it, indeed, be said that any one single difficulty—whether physiological or psychological—as regards brain, and nerves, and light, and images, and vibrations, and tympana, and labyrinths, and what not, has received solution at the hands of Hamilton? The position in the nervous system is, in effect, not only gratuitous but idle; and it is very characteristic of Hamilton that he should return in his metaphysical lectures to his dogged ὅτι, and wind up, though weakly enough, with such passages as:—

'But whether the senses be instruments, whether they be media, or whether they be only particular outlets to the mind incarcerated in the body,—on all this we can only theorise and conjecture.'

Nor is Hamilton one whit luckier in the step to his second net than in that to his first. This step is resistance—voluntary locomotion resisted; and from what we know now, it will not be difficult to perceive that the transition thence to a world without is capable of being met by the same principles which interposed beween the sensation proper and the perception proper. Resistance, that is, is but a subjective feeling, and how there should be any hint in it of an external object, constitutes the difficulty. Any mental experience, indeed, feeling or other, cannot be referred *out*, till there be an out known. Nor is it different with locomotion: this, too, would be simply a feeling, more or less intense, and would give no knowledge of movement till ideas of space and an external universe had been already formed; but for the formation of these ideas we find no competent provision supplied by Hamilton.

Hamilton, indeed, asserts direct perception of extension, and extension implies space; but as we have seen, he brings forward for himself no more than *assertion*; and we are compelled to indicate and demand the missing element of *proof*. The void between subjective sensation and objective perception he leaves unmediated; and we refuse to participate in the satisfaction he demands for his own mere spring. There are certainly times, however, when the simple recoil from intension to extension seems insufficient to Hamilton himself—times when, as it appears, he would really mediate between the intensive sensation of the membrane on the one side, and its extensive perception on the other. We have such deliverances as these, for example:—'Sensations out of each other, contrasted, limited, and variously arranged;' 'sensations recognised as plural, and reciprocally external;' 'sensations relatively localised;' 'all sensations, whatsoever, of which we are conscious, as one out of another, *eo ipso*, afford us the condition of immediately and necessarily apprehending extension.' Now, to judge from such expressions as these, there is more in the thought of Hamilton than that it is simply *fact*, that the sensation is the condition of the perception: he evidently contemplates something of *reason* as well. In other words, it is in the peculiar reciprocity of the sensations that he sees the prototype of extension. With this, too, his physiological ideas cohere: he would regard 'the ultimate fibrils as the ultimate units of sensation;' and he unequivocally attributes to 'the smaller size of the papillæ and fibrils of the optic nerve the greater power we possess, in the eye, of discriminating one sensation as out of another, and, consequently, of apprehending extension.' The theory that seems involved or desiderated, however, admits of a very simple refutation. The phrase, 'sensations one out of another,' can mean only one or other of two things: either sensations one out of another as different from one another; or sensations that, as such, have parts—that are, in their own nature, plural, out of one another, extended. Now, to take the latter alternative first, we have simply to point out that, in the matter of sensations, there are none such. Sensations are but subjective feelings; they possess intension not extension; and Hamilton has no authority to extend them to the latter. Physiologically there may be a certain breadth of surface affected, or, as in the eye, illuminated, and each nervous filament may correspond to a distinct unit of the sensation (light); but, psychologically, that is not so;—psychologically, it is the sensation (light) we know, and not the membrane; and this sensation (light), this subjective feeling, has degree, but not breadth.

Again, sensations out of one another, as different from one another, will give information of difference, but not of distance or separation—of different *quality*, but not of different *place*. If in different sensations, we find, not only difference of quality, but difference of place, then, evidently, this latter is something other than themselves—something that has been added to them. This, in fact, is one of Kant's strongest arguments for the original implication and primitive presupposition of space as an independent, *à priori*, or *pure perception*.

Without space, then, there is no possibility of a cognition on our part, whether of the first net on experience of a secondary quality, or of the second net (the outer world) on experience of what Hamilton calls a secundo-primary quality—resistance. Space is the indispensable, radical condition; and it is quite incapable of being deduced from any relation—reciprocal or other—of sensations. Nay, as we have seen already, the very attempt to derive a knowledge of space and the primary qualities—empirically—is, from the first, suicidal and absurd; and Hamilton's own sense of failure cannot help breaking out ever and anon in his own words. Even in the midst of reasonings about sensations reciprocally out of each other, he admits that space must be presupposed, else they would be reciprocally out of each other, only as different, but not as in different places; and, feeling, perhaps, the whole floor of natural realism thus sinking beneath him, he fairly gives way at last to a burst of ill-humour, as he exclaims:—' It is truly an idle problem to attempt imagining the steps by which we may be supposed to have acquired the notion of extension; when, in fact, we are unable to imagine to ourselves the possibility of that notion not being always in our possession!' It is quite characteristic, too, that, having thus given vent to his temper, and quite unconscious that he has at once supported, and demonstrated ignorance of, the relative doctrine of Kant, he can, in his stubborn mood, wind up:—' We have, therefore, a twofold cognition of space; a, an *à priori*, *native* imagination [not perception] of it in general, as a necessary condition of the possibility of thought [not experience]; and b, under that, an *à posteriori* or adventitious percept of it, &c.' [and thus he betrays unconsciousness that, to Kant, a and b are one and the same!]

In this way, then, it is patent that a physiological theory of the origin of our cognition of extension, whether placed in the position of the first net or in that of the second, is, from the very nature of the case, futile, and that Hamilton would have been only judicious had he saved himself this whole industry. An industry, indeed, that transfers the qualities of an unperceived and unknown organism to a perceived and known outer world in such wise that we only know what we do not know, while what we do not perceive is all that we do perceive, must be pronounced extravagant and improbable. Nor less objectionable is the violence which is done to consciousness in that it is transferred from the things without to the nervous tissue within, at the same time that its *natural* authority is claimed for it — in the new position — a claim which, on the part of Hamilton, can only vitiate his single appeal by demolishing the sole standard to which it is addressed, common sense. The interposition, indeed, of the nervous system between the mind within and the world without, which is the one act of Hamilton, must be declared, as it has been handled by him, supervacaneous and idle; not one difficulty affecting the intercourse of mind and matter having in reality been touched by it; while we are left at last with so insecure and insignificant a non-ego that we may legitimately conclude in regard to the general scheme of Hamilton, that it proves what it would disprove, and disproves what it would prove, or that it directly leads, not to presentative realism, but to cosmothetic idealism! Indeed, it is difficult to conceive any theory of perception more glaringly and thoroughly representative than that of Hamilton: that outer object, whatever it may be, that we suppose ourselves to perceive, is only in name an outer object; it is an unknown substrate, a phenomenon from the first, and we know it, not by what it presents, but by what it represents — the qualities, that is, primary and secondary, of our own nervous net, or, even, as in the case of the latter, of our own mental unit. It itself, the outer object, is never perceived at all—it is only *supposed*; and it is resistance, a state of our own, that thus supposes—that thus infers it. Nor is it for itself that it is inferred, but only for an *other*—only as *locus*, that is—only as place of reflections for qualities to which, whether primary or secondary, it itself may in no respect correspond. Any such correspondence as regards the latter class, Hamilton himself would seem to deny; and we cannot doubt now that, had he understood the evidence of Kant, he would have been similarly minded as regards the former. What universe, then, can we possibly conceive *more* representative? In Kant, the unknown outer substrate may be perceived at least to *harmonise* with the inner faculty; but we know of no provision in Hamilton for even so much presentationism as this. His primary qualities were at all times but an insignificant barrier against the great sea of relativity that existed for him everywhere else; but now that these are withdrawn, there is but a single expanse—an expanse of representationism—and its originator is Hamilton! *

* Hamilton, who would have inner immediate to outer, not only inserts *between* them the *medium* of the nerves, but in order still to effect imme-

Not only has the theory, however, a very ingenious look, especially at first hand, but it has also an original look; and we become curious to know how it was come by. Now, on this head, we may point out, in the first place, that what is now so commonly known as Berkeley's theory of vision, contains a very general analogy to the view in question. In both, what is held to be originally known by sight is but the lit or coloured ocular membrane; and in both, all that follows is but what has been called 'the art of seeing things that are invisible'—an art in which touch plays the tutor to sight, and teaches it to translate its own visual figure into its (the tutor's) tactual one. Now, Dr. Thomas Brown is generally admitted to have successfully controverted the assumption of visible figure as an original cognition of sight. To say, then, that Hamilton restored what Brown had destroyed, is not imperfectly to name Hamilton's whole action here. It was probably not from this direction, however, that Hamilton came on his theory;—though it is quite possible that it was at least partly from this direction that he came on his hatred to Brown. His theory once for all formed, that is, he conceivably found, to his astonishment, that Brown—and this is an experi-

diation, he is obliged to interpolate no less than eight contrivances more: the eight conditions, namely,—Attention, Quality, Space, Memory, Judgment, &c.,—which he assumes as necessary and indispensable to every act of perception. Such complicated mediacy contrasts oddly with the simple immediacy it would produce. Space is granted as a presupposition at last; but this presupposition, though it nullifies in advance, is not allowed to pretermit, the whole laborious theory. Then memory, which is representative to Hamilton himself, is a necessary element in what remains presentative all the same!

ence by no means the only one of the sort in the too precipitate Hamilton—had already destroyed it in advance.* Certainly *visible figure*, and *presence of the mind to its own organ*, do not, at first sight, look like synonyms, and it is this unlikeness which induces us to believe that the one was not derivative from the other; yet, beyond all doubt, synonyms they are, and the point of view thus obtained is crucial for the theory that contains the latter.

But, in the second place, the direction from which we believe Hamilton really to have come on his theory lies here:—At page 144 of his edition of Reid's *Works*, Hamilton refers to a comment by Stewart on a passage from Reid. The latter runs thus:—'Our eye might have been so framed as to suggest the figure of the object without suggesting colour or any other quality; and, of consequence, there seems to be no *sensation* appropriated to visible figure; this quality being suggested *immediately* by the material impression on the organ, of which impression we are not conscious.' The comment, again, after a declaration on the part of Stewart, that this has been a puzzle of forty years to him, is as follows:—'To my apprehension, nothing can appear more manifest than this, that

---

* Among the preceding objections to Hamilton's theory, perhaps the very strongest is that which points out that the metaphor of light is at once quenched when applied to the other senses. Consulting 'Brown's Lectures' in reference to Berkeley's theory of vision, I find that argument virtually anticipated by Brown; and yet I think I took it not from Brown, but from the nature of the case. One is rather gratified, however, by anticipations at the hands of a man like Brown, who is not only built into our admiration by his rare subtlety, but endeared to our very affection by his sweet candour.

if there had been no *variety* in our sensations of colour, and, still more, if we had no sensation of colour whatsoever, the organ of sight could have given us no information either with respect to figures, or to distance; and, of consequence, would have been as useless to us, as if we had been afflicted, from the moment of our birth, with a *gutta serena*.'

We may remark here, firstly, that Brown's general argument against the *originality* of visible figure as a cognition of sight, is, virtually, but a turning of the first averment of Reid against his second, or it is simply an inversion of the reasoning of Reid. Reid, namely (his thoughts being shaken into place), reasons thus:—Figure being different from, and no element of, the sensation colour, it must be *immediately suggested*. Brown, again, says, Figure being different from colour, and no element of the sensation, it can *not* be immediately suggested, but is acquired by experience of other sense.

Then, with reference to Stewart, surely he might have spared himself his long puzzle of forty years, seeing that the passage from Reid is nothing but an expression, not only of the general doctrine, but of the single argument, accepted by both, that the primary qualities, forming no part of the sensation, can only be *immediately suggested* on *occasion* of the sensation. Reid does not say that the eye *does* suggest figure without suggesting colour; he understands his own doctrine and its terms too well for that; but he says, ' The eye *might have been so framed*,' and it is, at least, usual to take these *might-have-beens*, especially where sense is concerned, necessarily idle though they be, with more equanimity than Stewart vouchsafes them.

But it is not with Stewart's forgetfulness of his own doctrine, and his consequent limitless absorption in speculation on the connection of colour and figure by a certain necessity, not only of fact, but of reason—which necessity of reason, did it exist (and it probably did exist to Hegel), would, by the *mediacy* it offered, destroy the *immediacy* attributed by himself to the cognition of the primary qualities—it is not with these aspects of Stewart that we are here concerned, but with this special averment of his in itself and in its special bearing on Hamilton's perceptive theory; of which theory surely it is at least capable of being regarded as the germ. For, not only does it declare the *perception* figure (the *objective* cognition) to be impossible without the *sensation* colour (the *subjective* passion), but it attributes to the *variety* of colour that same necessary, active, and positive function which Hamilton also attributes to the *variety* of colour, though under the name of *the relative localisation and reciprocal externality* of colours. The reflexion, or revulsion, of the mind from the subjective sensation to the objective membrane, this, indeed, is Hamilton's *salto mortale*, this is the centre of his theory, and it might quite possibly have been suggested by these passages which he himself signalises in Reid and Stewart.

But, as regards a theory so striking and so evidently the centre of his thought, if one be curious to know what suggested it, one is equally curious to know how it is that Hamilton has not given it all the prominence which his mastery of expression and his fervid personality might, had he so chosen, have so easily extended to it. For it is a remarkable fact that one shall have mastered the two volumes of the Logic, the two volumes of the Metaphysic, the one volume of the Discussions—that one shall have advanced far even into the text of the Dissertations to Reid—and yet that one shall remain absolutely blunt to the distinction in question until it suddenly dawn on him from the corner of some hardly readable, small-print footnote under these mentioned Dissertations. This is no solitary experience, and it is well-fitted to surprise. Nay, Hamilton's philosophical reading seems to have been undertaken for no other purpose than to give breadth to this distinction; yet, hardly mentioning it to his pupils, he allows it only a dark and stifled existence principally in foot-notes! We shall not attempt to account for this—we shall leave it simply to conjecture.

The reader who has now reached this centre of the nervous net will do well to turn round and survey the ground he has travelled. All, so, will be easier to him, and in readier proportion. The contradiction of presentationism and phenomenalism, the dogged ὅτι, the conversion of consciousness into perception, the unsatisfactory analysis of philosophy with its 3 or 4 of the external reality, &c.—all this, *as he now looks back on it from Hamilton's point of view*, will appear mitigated, and more natural. Nevertheless, all has been presented to him really as it strikes himself in Hamilton, and in that order which the interests of a full intelligence required. Nor, however softened the distant landscape may appear from the point we now occupy, is there a single dark spot the less in it; and we would remind summarily of the various objections to this point of view itself: 1. It is a *petitio principii* to begin with a nervous envelope, &c.—2. The theory is too predominatingly physiological.—3. The position of consciousness in the nervous net is not proved.—4. The entire *modus operandi* explains nothing, and the metaphor of light is but a delusion.—5. It is absurd to derive what is *à priori* from an *à posteriori* source.—6. It is extravagant to transfer out the nervous net in its sensations and in its perceptions as the entire outer universe.—7. It is to do violence to consciousness to transfer it from things it knows to nerves it knows not.—8. Such transference vitiates Hamilton's own appeal to consciousness.—9. The intercourse of mind and matter is as difficult as ever.—10. The theory performs on its self its own *Elenchus*—proving what it would disprove, and disproving what it would prove. Lastly, we would point out, in conclusion, that two of the above arguments are precisely those which convince himself of the erroneousness of that theory which derives the idea of *power* from a transference to outer objects of our own *nisus* in volition, namely, that there is no consciousness of the fact alleged (the presence of the mind to the net), and that even such consciousness would not yield the apodictic nature which the primary qualities bring with them.

4. *The Principle of Common Sense.*

It is manifest that some of the points just touched on are repugnant, as has been already hinted indeed, to the principles of common sense; and yet it is to common sense that Hamilton, in company with Reid, appeals; or it is in the name and interests of common sense that Hamilton, in the same company, works. Obviously, then, our review of the present subject will be only complete when we have carried it up into that complement of principles which constitute, by profession at least, both its motive and its measure.

Now, by its very name, common sense is a common property: it is no man's fee-simple to do with as he will; it is every man's universal privilege; it is no man's particular advantage. The first inference we have to make here, then, is, that no use of the name will justify any departure from the standard, no matter however much he who leaves may praise what he leaves or deny that he leaves.

Now Reid, in a passage which has received the impress of Hamilton himself, describes (Reid's *Works*, p. 302) the platform of common sense thus:—

We have here a remarkable conflict between two contradictory opinions, wherein all mankind are engaged. On the one side stand all the vulgar who are unpractised in philosophical researches, and guided by the uncorrupted primary instincts of nature. On the other side stand all the philosophers, ancient and modern; every man, without exception, who reflects. In this division, to my great humiliation, I find myself classed with the vulgar.

The court, then, before which Reid—with the express approbation of Hamilton—would arraign philosophy, cannot well be misunderstood; nor more the general situation. As proclaiming the criterion of common sense, Reid stands with 'the vulgar;' he is 'guided by the uncorrupted primary instincts of nature,' to which instincts it is no prejudice that they are 'unpractised in philosophical researches;' he finds himself opposed by 'all the philosophers, ancient and modern'—by 'every man, without exception, who reflects;' and he has no resource but to appeal from the latter to the former,—from the 'philosophers' to the 'vulgar,'—from every man, without exception, who reflects, to every man—presumably—without exception, who does not reflect.

Before passing specially to Hamilton, we may remark that the contradiction in itself, which destroys this statement, is sufficiently obvious. Reflection, thought, is the single instrument of truth; and we do not usually listen twice to any man who tells us, Reflection unexceptively says A, irreflection unexceptively says B, nevertheless it is irreflection that is right. But Reid not only thus negates himself by his own first word, he equally negates himself by his own first act. No sooner, indeed, has he called to us not to reflect, than he sets himself to reflect. If, alarmed at 'philosophy,' he had said, Philosophy is naught, let us return to our usual beliefs, that what we taste we taste, and what we touch we touch, and leave reflection, he would have been perfectly consistent with himself, and dispute there could have been none; but, when he proceeded, instead, to open inquiry into these beliefs—then, in an instant, the vulgar had fled, and there was only philosophy again—philosophy at all its old cobwebs—cheerful, hopeful, busy as ever.

With Hamilton, too, we can bring the matter to the same short issue. When perception, namely, withdrew from the world without, and transported itself to the nerves within, common sense refused to follow, and Hamilton found himself cut off from it by a chasm as wide and deep as that that, to Reid, separated the 'philosophers' from the 'vulgar.'

But we are not confined to what is indirect here. Hamilton, the very loudest for the sufficiency of common sense, is equally the loudest for its insufficiency also. He says (Reid's *Works*, p. 752):—

> In this country in particular, some of those who opposed it [common sense] to the sceptical conclusions of Hume, did not sufficiently counteract the notion which the name might naturally suggest; they did not emphatically proclaim that it was no appeal to the undeveloped beliefs of the unreflective many; and they did not inculcate that it presupposed a critical analysis of these beliefs by the philosophers themselves.

He goes on, indeed, to assert that their language sometimes warranted an opposite conclusion; and he names Beattie, Oswald, and even Reid, as examples.

Now, this is surely very simple, but, at the same time, very equivocal, procedure. Reid says that common sense and philosophy are directly opposed; and he would destroy the latter under the feet of the former. I quite agree with him, says Hamilton; I cry common sense too, but I practise philosophy all the same. That is, I take the name common sense—it is a good name; then 'I counteract the notion which it might naturally suggest;' after that, 'I emphatically proclaim that it is no appeal to the undeveloped beliefs of the unreflective many;' next, 'I inculcate that it presupposes a critical analysis of these beliefs by the philosophers themselves;' lastly, 'I, as a "philosopher," still with the name and all the advantages of the position claimed, set on my "critical analysis," and tell my findings.' There are other inferences here; but we, for our parts, ask only, In what respect this position differs from that of 'the ideal system,' from that of 'Descartes, Malebranche, Locke, Berkeley, and Hume,' to combat and confute which were the reason and the necessity of any resort to common sense at all?

In Hamilton's hands, in fact, common sense shows no difference whatever from philosophy, and the conclusion of the whole matter just is, that we are all to reason to the best of our ability, reason itself being sure to pull us up when wrong. Reason, in fact, has no standard but reason; and, with whatever disinclination, no one can refuse to keep his seat, so long as it is reason that drives. The sentence from Hamilton, in truth, is nothing else than the restoration to the judge reason of the chair into which the drudge common sense had been for an instant thrust. Nevertheless, this is a deliberate act of Hamilton, and he will be found (Reid's *Works*, p. 816) expressly dividing common sense into a 'philosophical form,' and a 'vulgar form'—quite unaware, apparently, that, thereby, he has taken the standard on himself, or that he has transferred that standard to philosophy, or that he has vitiated and undermined the standard, or that he has demonstrated it to be a standard incompetent to him.

But the term, common sense, is as yet quite general, and the position abstract; what are the particular principles by which Hamilton would introduce into the latter a concrete filling? These principles—at least, to take the profession of Hamilton—are understood in a word when we describe them as what are known to philosophy as our stock of primary truths. True, it is very difficult to make out what these truths are, if we trust to Hamilton; but not the less does he make words enough about them. The characteristic signs by which he would have us recognise them, he tells us, for instance, may (Reid's *Works*, p. 754) 'be reduced to four;—1°, their Incomprehensibility—2°, their Simplicity—3°, their Necessity and absolute Universality—4°, their comparative Evidence and Certainty.' Now, suppose we draw attention here to sign the third first. Well, these two terms, necessary and universal, have, by Kant, been included together in the single word apodictic (written by purists apodeictic); and they concern one of the most important and fertile distinctions in later philosophy.

Hume busied himself much with what has proved, not only the *fundamen* of German philosophy, but the angle of all philosophy else, probably for some time to come—the distinction, namely, between *mat*-

ters of fact, and *relations of ideas*. The former are, one and all of them, whatever we have *experienced*—whatever we know by *experience*: and *experience*, as *medium of knowledge*, is *sense*, principally *external*, but also, as understood by Locke and Kant, *internal*. The sun shines, stones fall, fire burns, wood floats, &c. &c. &c.; and the truth of all such propositions, or the *fact* they name, is only known by *trial*, and *trial* is but another word for *experience*. We have actually *experienced* the event, and—to signalise the shade between the two words—we can, at any time, *try* it. Of all such propositions, it is seen that they *are* true; but it is not seen that they *are necessarily*, or *must be*, true. That is, no *reason* is seen *why* they are true; and, consequently, what is the same thing, their contrary implies no contradiction, and is equally possible. The contraries, for example, the sun does not shine, stones do not fall, fire does not burn, wood does not float, &c. &c. &c., we know by experience, by trial, to be untrue; but they are not contradictions to thought, they are not impossible, they are still conceivable (as really, perhaps, some woods do not burn); and they depend wholly and solely on the state of the case, which is, once for all, *found* to be so and so and not otherwise. Now truths of this nature—the former class, the matters of fact—are named by Hume (with reference to their validity, or peculiar evidence) *contingent*, and by Kant (with reference to their source experience, to the *after the fact* that is in them) *à posteriori*.

The latter class, again, the relations of ideas, are

widely different; and, in the words of Hume, consist of 'every affirmation which is either intuitively or demonstratively certain.' Indeed, seeing that whatever is demonstratively certain rests at last on what is intuitively certain, we may withdraw the former as superfluous, and define relations of ideas to be, all affirmations that are intuitively certain. Of this class all the axioms and propositions of mathematics are examples. The whole is greater than its part, for instance: for the proof of this, we do not refer to experience, to trial; we do not say that it just is so, that this is just the fact; we know that it, not only *is* so, but *necessarily* is so; we know the *reason why* it is so; and we know that its contrary (the whole is not greater than its part) implies a contradiction, and is by necessity impossible. This class, then, with reference to their validity are named necessary and universal, or apodictic, truths, and (by Kant), with reference to their independence of sense—of any trial or experience of sense—as source (the *before the fact*, or the independence of the fact), *à priori* truths.

There is good reason for believing, we may remark, that Hume, in using the word *intuitive*, attached to it that *evidence, vision, insight*—that actual *perception* and *looking-at*—which Kant always had before him in the German word for intuition—*Anschauung*. Indeed, it is pretty certain that their common predecessor, Locke, entertained the same view. 'Many a one,' he says (Book iv. c. vii. s. 10), 'knows that one and two are equal to three, without having heard or thought on that or any other axiom by which it might be proved; and knows it as certainly as any other man knows that the whole is equal to all its parts, or any other maxim, and all from the same principle of *self-evidence*; the equality of those ideas being as *visible* and certain to him, without that or any other axiom, as with it,—it needing no proof to make it *perceived*.' On the other hand, it seems to have been Reid who, through his definition of intuitive propositions as 'propositions which are no sooner understood than they are believed,' has made almost universally current since his time a somewhat different sense of the word— the '*no sooner*,' that is, or the immediacy and instantaneousness, as it were the instinctivity, which it also implies.

Hume, then, had the actual perception that an intuition involves well before his mind, though it rose not up to him, perhaps, as that *express inspection* which Kant considered it. He had in mind, not the *instantaneousness* of the insight only, but this *insight* itself. Intuitive truths, then, are truths that are *seen*,—truths that are *seeingly* believed, not truths that, as incomprehensible, must be *unseen*, and, if believed, can only be *unseeingly* believed. That the straight line is the shortest, requires no proof; but, for all that, it wants not *evidence*; it is no incomprehensible truth that rests on a blind belief alone; it is not only believed to be true, but it is seen to be true.*

Hume further characterises these truths of the second class thus:—' Propositions of this kind are

---

* See Note at end.

discoverable by the mere operation of thought, without dependence on what is anywhere existent in the universe: though there never were a true circle or triangle in nature, the truths demonstrated by Euclid would for ever retain their certainty and evidence.' Here Hume plainly intimates, not only that he knows such truths to bring *evidence*, but to be also *à priori* —'discoverable by thought,' that is, without any reference to, or direct trial of, anything actually in nature. We may regard, indeed, the *à priori* of Kant to have taken birth in this passage of Hume. Probably we know now, then, something of the true nature of those primary truths to which Hamilton's third characteristic sign applies, and will be able to judge of his relative utterances.

Now, we have to point out at once that these four characteristic signs of Hamilton are enumerated by him as referring to all primary truths indiscriminately alike. Of this we cannot doubt. He expressly (Reid's *Works*, p. 743, *note*) affirms of 'the primary truths of *fact*, and of the primary truths of *intelligence* (the contingent and necessary truths of Reid),' that, though 'two very distinct classes of the original *beliefs* or *intuitions* of consciousness,' '*there appears no sufficient ground to regard their sources as different.*' After this, it is not difficult for us to understand that Hamilton, in what seems to have been almost his one action on the platform of common sense, saw no contradiction in asserting the cognition of a material non-ego to be a universal and necessary first principle —an apodictic *datum* of consciousness. But, of this one action, if the first half—the *postulate* of a *stationary* consciousness, namely—be absurd, no less absurd is the second, that would elevate into the universal, necessary, and *à priori* validity of a relation of ideas, the matter of fact which is contained in our contingent, sensuous, and *à posteriori* cognition of the material world.* Consider together the averments:—A straight line is the shortest, a straight line is not the shortest; and, There is a material non-ego, there is no material non-ego. The different validity is at once apparent. In truth, the two classes of evidence cannot be confounded; and Hamilton, whatever he may say about 'no sufficient grounds,' knows this well. In fact, there is hardly any distinction in Hamilton with which his reader is more familiar than that between *necessity* and *contingency*. He alludes to the successful application of it by Kant; in disparagement of Kant he points to it in Leibnitz; and he asserts for Reid in its regard—and again in disparagement of Kant, who in this shall have been 'indebted to Leibnitz'—'an original and independent discernment.' (It was plain for both Kant and Reid, in what was most familiar to both—Hume.)

But Hamilton is hardly more satisfactory in the remainder of his characteristic signs. Opposing the last to the first, for example, or even the second to

---

* That the cognition of a material non-ego is but empirical, requires no reference to authority; Reid, however, will be found to enumerate it among his *contingent* primary truths. (Reid's *Works*, p. 441.) Hamilton probably lays weight, as already said, on the complete generality of the non-ego; but there is no more reason for declaring consciousness inviolable as regards the general fact of a material non-ego, than as regards the movement of the sun, or the crookedness of an immersed stick.

the first, and having always understood that *evidence*, especially if *simple*, is precisely that by which incomprehensibility becomes comprehensibility, we are at a loss to conceive how the same thing that is *incomprehensible* should be, not only *simple*, but *evident*.

The discrepancy contained in the enumeration, then, is certainly bad enough; but it is probably outdone by that in the paragraph that follows it, where Hamilton tells us that that of which we know, not only *that* it is, but also *how* or *why* it is, 'is not a primary datum of consciousness, but a subsumption under the cognition or belief which affords its reason.' The ordinary axioms, then, seeing that they always bring their own *why*, are henceforth on the authority of Hamilton to be conceived to be excluded from the rank of primary data! The law of contradiction itself, though set up by Hamilton himself as—so to speak—the very first primary of all primaries, must, seeing that it too brings its own evidence, consent to be thrown down again, and by the hand that set it up. Nay, the same authority, who formerly declared a thing—because of its *evidence*—to be primary, now declares it—and still because of its evidence—*not* to be primary.

There are many passages in Hamilton where the insight, which is contained in the etymology of the word *intuitive*, is noticed; but, on the whole, his custom is pretty much the same as Reid's: he correlates (as we have seen, p. 119) *intuition* with *belief*, and considers the *instantaneousness* of the intuition rather than the intuition itself. It is to this we attribute the discre-

pancies and confusions which have been just exposed.*
But attribute them to what we may, anything more
piebald and unequal than this their resulting or em-
bracing doctrine of common sense we do not believe
to exist. It is common sense, yet the natural meaning of the phrase is to be counteracted, and it is not
to be common sense. It is common sense, yet the
result—of *analysis*—*critical* analysis—and by the
philosophers. It is common sense, but not the sense
of the common (the vulgar); it is the sense of the
uncommon (the philosophers). Then its constitutive
principles, they are incomprehensible yet evident, inconceivable yet 'clear,' nay 'the *light* of nature;' they
are contingent yet necessary, particular yet universal,
à posteriori yet *à priori*, products of sense yet products
of intelligence. Finally, this loose shelf of principles,
whose origin we know not, whose connexion we know
not, whose completion we know not—principles which
have been come upon and taken up we know not how,
principles which lie apart and mutually indifferent,
principles which coalesce not into the unity of a
system, principles which are not even assigned—
finally, we say, this loose shelf of pêle-mêle, un-
vouched principles is set identical with the—*Reason*

* Hamilton (*Logic*, i. 126) says: 'This expression [intuition as a looking at] has, however, been preoccupied in English to denote the apprehension we have of self-evident truths, and its application in a different significa-tion [the perceptive] would, therefore, be, to a certain extent, liable to ambiguity.' This, with reference to the vision present in intuitive truths, would read like an excuse for not using intuition in its perceptive sense, because it is already preoccupied in that sense! Evidently, then, the *instinct* of the intuition has shut out from Hamilton's view the *insight* of it. See also page 171 same work, where he seems to have in view the *speed* of the looking rather than the looking.

of Kant (the objects of which are God, Freewill, and the Soul)!—and distinguished from the—*Understanding* of Kant, the objects of which are just those very principles which (the roots and foundations of human knowledge) constitute, as *named* (they are not *given*), Hamilton's special quest here! What strange effect, indeed, to compare this loose shelf (with but a stray specimen on it all the same) with the one organic germ of Kant, in which lie vitally complete a whole co-articulated congeries of constitutive members! But why mention Kant?—It was Hamilton's pride to have perfected the presentationism of Reid—to have strengthened into impregnability his fortress of common sense: in reality, he has but overthrown the one, and broken up the other!

But it is just possible that any conclusion yet is premature; for it is now in place to recollect that Hamilton does not stop with common sense, but carries all up into a so-called—Law of the Conditioned. This we have now to see.

NOTE (*See* p. 118).

'Kant held the *intuitive* cognition of *outness*:' this has been said in this country, and it would have been right if the *sayer* had meant, Kant held space to be *perceptive*. It is illustrative of what has been said above, however, to consider that the sayer really meant only something that was somehow mysteriously *instantaneous* or *instinctive*. We, Scotch, have made ourselves simply ridiculous by the mystic *hocus-pocus* we have somehow *imaginatively* conjured into the word *intuitive*, instead of merely seeing and saying that it was tantamount to *perceptive*. 'Kant does not give the Intuitions'—'I give the Intuitions!' it is curious to realise to oneself the strange magical functions of our own secret inner which are supposed, in such words, to be, as it were, weirdly seen into through vapour, and by means of some supersensuous, quite original insight. Pure intuitions, however, there are none, but the pure *perceptions* Time and Space. Apperception, Self-consciousness, the Ego, the inner One, is *externalised* into the net of the *categories* (as functions if you will); these into the net of the *intuitions*, Time and Space; and these, again, into the ultimate net of *actual empirical things*. And what we have *so* is, *this* world, the proper name of which is *Spirit*—Free and Immortal Spirit—Spirit in communication with Spirit—Spirit in dependence on, and in reconciliation through Christ with, the one Absolute Spirit—God.

This, I take it, is pretty nearly the Kantianism of Hegel; and it is Kantianism, and nothing but Kantianism, that is the *matter* assimilated by Hegel as food and *filling*, into his own *form*.

www.ingramcontent.com/pod-product-compliance
Lightning Source LLC
Chambersburg PA
CBHW021937160426
43195CB00011B/1124